DO YOUR OWN HOME STAGING

Tina Parker

Self-Counsel Press
(a division of)
International Self-Counsel Press Ltd.
USA CANADA

Self-Counsel Press acknowledges the financial support of the Government of Canada through the Book Publishing Industry Development Program (BPIDP) for our publishing activities.

Printed in Canada.

First edition: 2009

Library and Archives Canada Cataloguing in Publication

Parker, Tina

  Do your own home staging / Tina Parker.

  Accompanied by a CD-ROM.

  ISBN 978-1-55180-838-3

  1. Home staging. 2. House selling. 3. Interior decoration.
  I. Title.

HD1379.P37 2008   643'.12   C2008-906241-8

Information on moving with animals in Chapter 8 provided with permission by The Humane Society of the United States; for more information on moving with animals visit the website at www.hsus.org.

Every effort has been made to obtain permission for quoted material and illustrations. If there is an omission or error, the author and publisher would be grateful to be so informed.

This book is printed in Canada on 100% post consumer waste
Forest Stewardship Certified recycled paper, using plant-based inks.
The paper is processed chlorine free and manufactured using biogas energy.

Self-Counsel Press
(a division of)
International Self-Counsel Press Ltd.

1704 North State Street	1481 Charlotte Road
Bellingham, WA 98225	North Vancouver, BC V7J 1H1
USA	Canada

CONTENTS

APPENDIX I — GENERAL CHECKLISTS

APPENDIX II — HOME IMPROVEMENT CHECKLISTS

APPENDIX III — HOME STAGING CHECKLISTS

ACKNOWLEDGMENTS

The most sincere thank you to my soul mate, the father of my two wonderful boys, for without your support and encouragement I could not have succeeded in writing this book or following my dreams.

Thank you to Tracy Moore of Montreal, Quebec, and Karen Otto of Home Star Staging, Plano, Texas, for your editing expertise, suggestions, and encouragement.

NOTICE TO READERS

FOREWORD

YOU HAVE ONE CHANCE TO MAKE A FIRST IMPRESSION

After selling real estate for several years, I found myself searching for new ways to set myself apart from other agents. I tried different marketing tools before deciding to attempt the new and still fresh method of home staging. Home staging was, and still is, misunderstood by many agents. After several interviews and meetings with prospective home stagers, I happened upon Tina Parker. I was immediately drawn to Tina and her enthusiasm towards her work. She was the only stager that I got a genuine feeling of competency from.

I have often entered a home and felt that the house was beautiful and showed extremely well, and yet I would still feel that something was missing and be unable to pinpoint the issue. Tina's innate ability to convey her knowledge of home staging concepts to both myself and home owners allowed me to uncover and resolve these issues, and therefore market properties to a wider range of clients. These homes often sold closer to their list prices with reduced time on the market. By staging a home prior to listing it, sellers can have a positive impact on the market immediately, as opposed to taking a "let's see what happens" approach. The latter marketing blunder often stigmatizes a home and allows initial prospects to slip away.

The best home stagers can not only picture how the room will appear the most attractive, but can also create a lifestyle for prospective buyers. Homes will be judged by how they look and how they feel, which means that both are a part of setting its market value. The market value of a home is set by the buyer. Most home owners expect top dollar for their home; however, they are not willing to put in the time, effort, or money needed to make the property marketable. Many will take the initiative to paint and decorate the home to their tastes, but will ultimately choose the wrong colors and furniture placement. Individual styles vary, so it is invaluable to draw on the resources of someone who studies the market and knows what buyers are looking for. Home staging will keep your home fresh and ahead of the competition.

I have used Tina's services consistently and with great success for the last few years. She is very creative and insightful, and can make the smallest of rooms look large and the darkest of rooms look bright. I have always said, "You have one chance to make a first impression." After using Tina's services, I realize you can stage your home to make the best possible first impression.

This book is an invaluable resource for anyone selling a home. It is an investment that you will not regret.

Sherry Shaddock

HOW HOME STAGING CHOSE ME

I am naturally a creative thinker, who constantly comes up with solutions to challenges and ideas for how to do things better. I cannot help it. There are four or five ideas developing in my mind at any given time!

My ability to create was nurtured as a young child; I started learning about scale, color, texture, balance, and composition at the age of five. I primarily used pencil or charcoal to draw people and landscapes in intricate detail, but I also used sculpture, etching, and painting as creative outlets. Throughout my life I've applied these skills to various experiences in order to see both the details and the big picture.

Although I chose an education in marketing and have worked in various industries, my passion for home improvement and interior decorating led me to use my creativity throughout the years to solve challenges my friends and family had in their homes. I jumped at opportunities to use my talents and gain valuable knowledge of home decor through various experiences working with and helping others. It wasn't until I owned my own homes, however, that I really thrived on the before and after results of home improvement and began to use these skills to make a considerable profit.

I am excited that the act of getting a home ready for a quick sale now has an identity. Home staging puts to use my creativity, talent, passion, education, and work experience; some of which includes interior decorating, home improvement, target marketing and consumer demographics, consumer relationship management, and graphic design. All of these factors have come together to successfully support and develop my home staging business, which I started after I acquired my Certified Staging Professional designation in April 2006.

The opportunity to take a product such as real estate and develop it into a hot commodity to sell in today's intelligent marketplace is exciting. Every property is different and provides various challenges that require me to develop creative solutions. Every project requires strategy, creative process, enthusiasm for challenges, and the desire to help sell each property as though it is my own. Home staging and I are a perfect fit.

CHAPTER 1

MAXIMIZE YOUR CHANCES FOR SUCCESS:
Make the Most of This Book

In 2007 I put the ideas and concepts of this book into action and sold my home within three days, for 98 percent of the asking price. The best part of my experience was the confidence I felt when it went onto the market. I had peace of mind; I knew it would sell fast, and I found the whole process relatively easy and stress free.

This book is designed specifically with you in mind: the average, busy, working person. I am married and have two active young boys, I volunteer, and I run a successful business — so I know what busy is too. I provide reasonable advice on how to best prepare a home for the market. I don't tell you to do anything I could not do myself. This book contains everything that I advise clients, including creative ideas, solutions, and suggestions for how to acquire the basic skills required to carry out the work.

My approach to preparing a home for sale has always been a combination of proven staging techniques and target marketing strategies. After all, you are selling a product. You don't need to be a professional to stage a home, but you do need to be a little bit creative. If you have physical restrictions, no access to help, or challenges (as described later in the book), you may want to seek assistance from professionals. It won't cost you any money if you figure in what you'll save if you hire them.

This book will also give you all of the information, tips, techniques, and checklists that you need to bring your house up to today's high market expectations. You can either use the checklists provided in the appendixes or print out copies from the enclosed CD, and use them as you follow this book. You may find it helpful to organize everything in a binder so you can keep track of what you need to do during the process of selling your house and moving to your next home.

The Sequence of Events in the Home Staging Process

There is no way for anyone to write out a complete priority list to help you with the complicated task of prepping your home for sale, because there are so many variables that can change or may be unique to you and your family.

The best way to make this transition as stress free as possible is to make an effort to be flexible. Flexibility is the key to overcoming any challenges that may come your way. The following priority list is put together to offer you some guidance and to help you navigate through the staging process:

- Read through this book completely before you begin, to get a good idea of the tasks required during the process.

- Put on your "buyer's eyes" and complete your "Home Improvement Checklists," available in Appendix II and on the CD. The home improvement part of the process can take quite some time, depending on the size of your home and the amount of work that needs to be done. The checklists are designed so that you can use a new list for each room, to ensure that you are thorough. Take advantage of the time you spend in each room and consider what your target market may be interested in. Decide if you want to invest in your house to maximize its value and to

increase the chances of selling it faster.

- Next, use the "Home Staging Checklists," available in Appendix III and on the CD. It will also be helpful if you write down your own ideas that are specific to your house as you go through the process.

- At this point, your to-do list and the rest of your "General Checklists" (available in Appendix I and on the CD) may seem overwhelming, but they will help you organize everything you need to do.

- Then, pack everything you will not be using in the next six to nine months. Enlist some help as de-cluttering and pre-packing are big jobs. See Chapter 8, "Packing and Moving Tips," for more suggestions.

- Your home will then be ready to stage. Proven ideas and techniques listed in Chapters 4, 5, and 6 can now be implemented.

- Once you feel that you have successfully prepared your home for the market, check your "Home Staging Checklists" again to determine if there is anything you have overlooked. Sketch furniture arrangements on the "Furniture Layout Grid" supplied in Appendix I and on the CD to figure out the best way to provide an effective traffic flow. Often, you can get a better idea of a room's traffic flow when viewing it from above.

- Ideally, it is at this point that you will call your real estate agent to provide you with an accurate market analysis.

Your agent can provide you with the best possible price for your house because you will already have highlighted the home's best features and eliminated many of the key obstacles buyers use to chip away at your asking price.

- If you chose to stage your house after it was put on the market, it would be a good idea to invite your real estate agent back, so he or she can realize its greater potential and take new pictures to put on the cut sheet and the Internet.

- In order to maintain the level of excellence you've worked so hard to achieve in your home, keep your "Open House Checklist" (available in Appendix I and on the CD) close by at all times.

- Relax for the moment, because before long, you'll be moving. To help set priorities relating to the big move, read Chapter 8, "Packing and Moving Tips."

CHAPTER 2

UNDERSTANDING HOME STAGING

One can say, without a doubt, that the process of selling real estate has changed over the past decade to include home staging. Today's marketplace is well-informed, educated, very particular, and accustomed to experiencing great customer service when purchasing products — especially when buying high-ticket items. Technology has changed how real estate is promoted, as 84 percent of potential home buyers are looking to the Internet to find properties. Photographs are the new first impression, instead of curb appeal. Besides showing what a room looks like, photographs tell a story and sell a lifestyle or feeling about a home.

Preparing your home with home staging will allow you to use these first impressions to your best advantage before any actual viewings. The home staging techniques described in this book are effective tools for increasing your chances of selling your property faster and for more money.

What is Staging?

In general, everyone looks for comfort, adoration, status, and excitement in life, all of which are involved in the psychology of buying a home. Successful staging capitalizes on these feelings and creates an ambiance that compels people to take their time and imagine themselves living in the space. Essentially, staging maximizes a home's potential to encourage the buyer to put in an offer.

Staged homes—

- sell two to three times faster,

- sell for 3 percent to 10 percent more money,
- look better in photos and marketing promotions,
- attract more buyers and more offers,
- eliminate buyers chipping away at the asking price,
- show your level of commitment to your real estate agent,
- prepare you for moving to your new location, and
- assure you that you've secured the best possible deal.

The Developing Industry of Home Staging

Before home staging became commonplace in real estate, it was primarily used as a last resort; if a home did not sell within a specified time, a professional home stager was called in. Home staging grew in popularity because homes sold quickly after being staged and, quite frequently, attracted amounts close to their asking prices. Eventually, it became normal practice for real estate agents to suggest various tips for preparing a home for sale, mostly de-cluttering and a good cleaning.

As the home staging industry grew, it became known for more than just de-cluttering and cleaning. More and more, real estate agents were paying attention to the effectiveness of staging a home, and it was the forward-thinking agents who called in professional home stagers to prepare homes before they went onto the market. Doing so made their listings look far better than their competitions' and practically guaranteed that their properties would sell before others in the same neighborhood. Forward-thinking home owners also had the foresight to see that home staging maximized the market value and increased the equity of their property.

Home staging is a young, self-regulated industry and has only recently begun to develop. New home staging training companies are forming rapidly every day. The Real Estate Staging Association (RESA) was formed as an industry-wide trade association in 2007. Its mission is to cultivate industry-wide standards for all stagers, regardless of their training, certifications, designations, or backgrounds. It also provides support and continuing education to maintain a level of excellence in the industry. You can find out more by visiting the website: www.realestatestagingassociation.com.

RESA conducted a study on properties that were professionally staged from January 2007 to February 2008 and found remarkable results. RESA looked at the amount of time non-staged, marketed properties spent on the market without selling, and compared that to the amount of time these same properties spent on the market when both staged and marketed. In one case, homes that spent 120 days on the market unstaged (without ever selling), sold after only 26 days when staged. In another, homes that spent 102 days on the market unstaged (without ever selling), sold after only 45 days when staged. RESA also found that vacant homes sold on average 40 days after staging, while occupied homes sold on average 38 days after staging.

Fast forward several years from now and home staging will be a prerequisite for selling a property, much like the home inspection industry, which we barely had 15 years ago. Potential home buyers will come to expect to view properties that have been staged and will walk away from those that have not been staged.

Marketing Strategies Behind Home Staging

Marketing has evolved over the past century to reflect developments in society. It has continued to advance in the direction that it shifted to in the '70s, which was from consumers buying what was produced, to consumers telling producers what to make.

As time passed this marketing practice became "normal" and producers had to compete to make the customer happy, which resulted in lower prices for products. It was not until these lower prices became the norm that relationship marketing became the next approach to making a customer happy. Today's culture has been greatly influenced by the relatively new information-technology industry, which has created higher expectations for faster, better, and personalized service. This increase in marketplace expectations has made customers anticipate a pleasant experience along with their purchase.

As a result of these evolving buying habits, there have been two major shifts in the approach to selling real estate; agents now recognize that people want "move-in ready" homes as well as "an experience."

Today most families and young professionals are trying to balance work, never-ending education, busy personal lives, and debt. Members of our society just don't have the time they once had. Increasing pressure to do more, get more, and pay more has created this shift in demand for a property that is move-in ready.

Consider these two lifestyle examples. The first is a family of four with two working parents and two school-aged children who are involved in activities. The cost of living, activities, and raising the children in an image-conscious society can put an overwhelming financial demand on a family. Time is precious, and tackling home improvements is not likely to be on their list of priorities.

The second is a young professional couple, recently graduated, and likely burdened with post-education debt, the demands of their new professions, and the never-ending education required to sustain them. Also, Generation Y is less likely to have a strong skill set for doing home improvements, so it is more likely that they would have to hire someone to get the work done.

These examples are common and demonstrate why home buyers desire move-in ready homes.

Relationship marketing

Technology, including the ease of the Internet, is the second major influence on the recent changes in buying habits; it has created higher service expectations and set the stage for relationship marketing, which provides the "experience" the customer is looking for.

For example, going to the salon to get a haircut used to involve sitting in a chair and having your hair sprayed with water to prepare it for cutting. Then it evolved into having your hair washed and conditioned to prepare it to be cut, dried, and styled. Take a trip to a hair salon today, and you will most likely be greeted with an offer to hang up your coat and an invitation to enjoy a free beverage while you wait. You will spend time in the chair discussing your expectations with the hairdresser, then you will be led to the hair washing station where you will receive a head massage as the hair conditioner sets. You will experience your cut, dry, and style in a relaxed environment, as opposed to the hurried one you once knew. When leaving the salon you will make your next appointment and hope that you won't forget it, but not to worry, the salon will call you two days beforehand to remind you. Altogether, the salon will provide you with a much better experience than it used to, and try to ensure that you will return to them, the people that made you feel good and established your trust. This is relationship marketing.

In brief, relationship marketing is establishing long-term, trusting relationships with customers in order to satisfy them so that they return, rather than shop around for their next purchase. As a result of this increased level of customer service, it is only natural for buyers to anticipate "an experience" with their purchases.

How is this relevant to home staging? It is important to realize that although you only have one product to sell, it is the potential buyer's expectation of "an experience" that will ultimately influence his or her decision whether or not to purchase your house. Similarly, home staging will create an atmosphere that allows potential buyers to experience or imagine living in the house at its best. Home staging strategies have been developed from an understanding of both relationship and target-marketing practices and ensure that you sell your house quickly and for more money.

Target marketing

To increase your chances of a quick sale, you will need to broadly market your house and appeal to various potential buyers. How you do this depends on the "identity" of your home, which is defined by its location, style, and features.

Location will attract various types of potential buyers; for example, an elementary school in the neighborhood will attract a young family, but a shopping district in a downtown location will typically attract young professionals.

The style of the home is also a major factor. A new, modern home with the latest in technologies will likely attract highly educated, young professionals. In contrast, a 20th-century Victorian home will attract the typical Generation X folk, because they are old enough to have their education debt paid off; have more confidence in their ability to tackle home improvements; have more time because their children are older; and have an annual income that is in its prime. The vast difference is evident in that Baby Boomers come from a generation of hard work, appreciation of quality, and an acceptance that with a house purchase comes work. Those of a younger generation typically favor things that satisfy their need for instant gratification; they aren't necessarily exposed to as much physical hard work as the older generation may have been; and they expect a move-in ready home that doesn't require any immediate work.

The style of decor can also be an issue, as having your favorite color on the walls will not appeal to those who dislike the color, or those who do not have the time, energy, or money to have it painted.

Various features will also attract particular buyers. For example, a landscaped backyard that has a pool and a patio designed as an outdoor room will attract either a couple who love to entertain or a family with teens or older children. In contrast, families with young children will often fear a pool because of its potential danger, and older couples looking to simplify their lifestyle will often not be interested. Many preferences are related to the buyer's age and income, such as young buyers purchasing their first home versus older buyers looking to trade down (perhaps in anticipation of retirement), while some features tend to be embraced by all home buyers. Other preferences will depend on how long the buyer expects to remain in the home. The desirability of certain features is also reflected in the buyer's choice between a new or a previously owned home.

Understanding who will be interested in your home helps you stage it so that it appeals to the majority of potential buyers. For example, imagine that you are selling a saltbox (a colonial, wood-framed house) in a suburban neighborhood that includes local amenities and an elementary school. The house is large enough to accommodate future needs, its layout suits a family, and it's located in a safe neighborhood that has amenities nearby and is close enough to school that the kids can walk. In this case, it is likely that your house will attract a family with young children; therefore, it would be in your best interest to market the property to appeal to this target market. This can be achieved by understanding how certain demographics typically perceive life and what their preferences are in terms of lifestyle.

This means that home owners looking to sell should invest in upgrading specific areas of the home, arranging furnishings, and displaying items that will represent the potential buyer's ideal lifestyle, regardless of how they themselves lived in the house and their personal taste in decor.

You could consider upgrading key features of the kitchen such as the flooring, cabinet hardware, countertop, sink, and faucet. Or you can change the third bedroom from its current office arrangement back to a bedroom, but stage it as a young child's room. Even if your children are grown and there are only two of you left in the house, staging it to attract your target market will increase your chances of receiving an offer.

Remember, most buyers use their hearts as well as their minds when shopping for a

While it is often said (perhaps preached is a better word) that staged homes must be neutral in order to appeal to the masses, we find that bringing in the bling with color in the form of accessories is the simple step that catches the eye and the offer. We can go one step further and work the color angle as it is matched to the target market. For example, the retiree crowd may be more attracted to warm yet subdued colors, while the young family will be more open to what we think of as Crayon® colors with bright red, yellow, and blue as the basics.

Yvonne Root
rooms b.y. root, AZ

new house, so appeal to their emotions. You can find additional specific recommendations in the following chapters.

Developing Your Staging Strategy

There are various occasions when you might need to stage your entire home, but sometimes you will only need to stage a couple of rooms to sell a desired lifestyle. A staging strategy starts with developing an identity for your home and understanding where your house is situated in the marketplace.

Take an objective look around your neighborhood. Who would be most attracted to the area? Are there schools nearby? If so, what level? Are there shopping malls, fitness centers, nature parks, playgrounds, or skating rinks? You get the idea. Do not assume that potential buyers will be interested in your home for the same reasons that you were. The neighborhood could have changed for better or for worse or expanded to include facilities that weren't previously there, and businesses could have evolved to accommodate different target markets such as seniors, families with young children or teenagers, singles, or couples with no children. All of these factors need to be considered.

Also take an objective look at the best features of your home to help you determine who would be most attracted to it. Does it have a large kitchen, a swimming pool, a large fenced backyard, a private tree-lined yard, a master bedroom with a bathroom and a walk-in closet, or four or two bedrooms? Keep these features in mind when considering how you will stage your home.

If there is a high school, shopping mall, or arcade nearby, stage the house to attract families with teenagers. Arrange the recreation room or family room as though teenagers live in the home. No, I do not mean piling clothes on the floor and putting posters on the walls. What I do mean is that you should borrow or buy items of interest to teens (if you do not already have them) and incorporate them into your home. Arrange your furniture for watching movies or playing electronic games, and perhaps place textbooks neatly on the coffee table or bookcase. Use your imagination — you may be surprised with what you can do! The space doesn't need to look exactly as though someone in your target market really lives there, but your staging should suggest that the home would be a suitable choice for them.

The Key to Selling Quickly and for More Money

If you are like most home owners, you are emotionally invested in your home. You've poured a lot of love, sweat, and tears — not to mention money — into personalizing it to suit your own tastes and needs. However, if you want to sell your home quickly and for the largest sum possible, you'll need to allow your potential buyers to imagine their own personalized vision of the space. Years of home ownership can foster strong emotional ties, and often, an initial hurdle to staging is detaching from these emotions. Begin to look at your home as a "house"; in other words, as a commodity, and as a product that needs to appeal to a wide market in order to sell quickly.

Most buyers rely on their hearts in addition to their minds when buying a new house. This is because they are not just buying a home, they are also buying into a dream or a lifestyle. If you leave it up to their imaginations to envision their dreams when they view your home, you are risking that they might not see any indication of the lifestyle they are looking for. If you use staging to guide their vision, you will influence how they feel in the home, which will have an effect not only on the number of offers, but also on the final sale price.

Preparing your home for sale is like dating!

I remember when I was single and looking for a soul mate to share my life with. You know: the dating scene. You send out smoke signals, tell people, maybe even place an ad in the newspaper or online that you are searching for a mate. You get several people interested in meeting you based on the characteristics they are seeking in a mate. You find someone you have things in common with — he or she may be what you are looking for!

Great, you're excited! You're getting ready for a date. Do you leave the house in your roughed-up jeans, with messy hair, wearing no makeup or cologne, and perhaps in need of a shower? NO! You get cleaned up, put on your best clothing and pretty yourself up the best you can with what you've got to work with. The potential mate meets you at a nice place and likes what he or she sees. You're on your best behavior and display your most positive side. You talk positively and are positive about the future. Are you this positive all the time? Absolutely not, but he or she doesn't have to know that on the first date. By now, he or she likes this first impression of you.

It is up to you to show your positive side, your lovable character, and your special features until this person falls in love with you. Then, and only then, do you show a little more of your negative side — which will be okay, because he or she loves you. If you show your negative side during your first or second date, he or she will run for the hills because he or she is not in love with you and cannot overlook your flaws.

The same principles apply when selling your home. Show off your home's best features, make it look its best, make sure everything is functioning properly, and make potential buyers feel at home. Remember, if they feel at home, they will BUY your home!

Why invest in a house you are leaving?

There are several reasons why you should invest in a house you are leaving. For example the marketplace is demanding move-in ready homes, the generation gap has created higher

 A 2004 survey by Joy Valentine — Coldwell Banker Broker, on 2,772 homes in 8 cities, found that staged homes sold in 13.8 days, while homes that were not staged sold in 30.9 days. Even more convincing is the fact that the staged homes realized on average a 6.4 percent increase over the list price!

expectations, real estate is an investment to protect, and, by investing in your home it will sell more quickly and for more money.

When real estate agents were asked how much they thought staging increased the value of a property (in HomeGain's 2007 national survey), 9.78 percent said $0–$1000; 11.96 percent said $1001–$2500; 29.35 percent said $2501–$5000; and 48.91 percent said $5001+! This is especially important when you take into account the 2005 and 2006 Maritz Research staging polls' finding that 79 percent of sellers are willing to spend up to $5,000 to get their house ready for sale.

As mentioned earlier, most of today's families and young professionals expect a beautiful and functional home, yet they don't have much, if any, time to spend on home repairs. In previous decades, home buyers expected that they would need to take care of repairs, maintenance, and painting in order to get the home of their dreams. Buyers were also more likely to have the necessary tools and knowledge to make changes to houses with potential, which allowed them to buy with confidence. However, this is not the case with the majority of buyers today, who may require or demand a move-in ready home. The Maritz

Research polls also found that 63 percent of buyers are willing to pay more for a move-in ready house!

Therefore, updating, repairing, and painting are necessary for preparing your house for sale in today's marketplace. If not, you may have to wait a long time to find that rare buyer who knows how to see past existing challenges, such as outdated light fixtures, purple or dirty walls, green carpet, or dented moldings — all seemingly easy fixes, but not for those who aren't imaginative or don't have time for home repairs.

To protect your investment and maximize the value of your home, invest in small upgrades such as new countertops, faucets, light fixtures, flooring, and fresh paint. In fact, the Maritz Research polls found that the top three interior features for selling are freshly painted walls, organized storage space, and current flooring. If your house is up for sale in an area with other similar listings, your house will sell faster than those that have not addressed the features that will make them a competitive listing. Think about this. Your competition may have purchased this book as well.

CHAPTER 3

HOME IMPROVEMENTS

Home improvements are an important step in making sure that your house is ready to stage and sell. Since all homes will have different needs, follow the "Home Improvement Checklists" (available in Appendix II and on the CD) to make sure you've covered all the bases for your property.

Ten Recession-Proof Home Improvements

A 2008 poll of registered voters by The American Institute of Architects (AIA) revealed that 90 percent of respondents would be willing to pay $5,000 more for a house that would use less energy and protect the Earth. According to the AIA survey, the following home improvement products have increased in demand (even in hard times).

ENERGY STAR windows

Paying more for ENERGY STAR certified windows will save you money in the long run. There are also many purchasing incentives and rebates available. Although most houses will benefit from energy-efficient windows, the further north you reside the more you will enjoy the annual savings in heating costs. See www.energystar.gov.

To find out more, visit the US Environmental Protection Agency website (www.epa.gov), if you are in the US, or the Office of Energy Efficiency website (www.oee.nrcan.gc.ca) if you are in Canada.

Water-saving toilets

Water conservation is important in today's eco-conscious world, and water-saving toilets can play a large role in trimming down a home's water use. While most standard toilets use 3.43 gallons or 13 liters of water per flush, water-saving toilets usually use less than 1.32 gallons or 5 liters!

Water heater

Traditional water heaters will heat water constantly, but there are various models available that only heat water as needed. Since these work on demand, you'll never run out of hot water! And, in most cases, a more energy-efficient system will pay for itself in just one year.

Radiant heat

Radiant heat is a technology whereby radiant energy is emitted from an element such as the floor or wall. The US Department of Energy estimates that radiant heating is 20 percent more efficient than conventional heating systems and can save you 20 percent per year in heating costs.

Landscaping

A landscaped yard with a garden not only provides great curb appeal and health benefits, it also gives buyers their first impression of a home. If your front yard discourages people before they even view the house, you are in trouble.

Doorless showers

The doorless shower is the best alternative to the traditional model, and is a design trend that builders and architects mention again and again as something consumers want. Also called walk-in showers, the enclosure is popular among aging Baby Boomers. Since

baths require more water, there are increased numbers of buyers looking for more eco-friendly bathing options.

Cork floors

As an alternative to tile and wood-plank flooring (which is pricier), low-density cork flooring is an effective insulator, does not rot when exposed to water, and does not absorb dust. Premium cork flooring can run at about $6.75 per square foot, assuming that you are looking to cover 600 or more square feet.

Bamboo countertops

Bamboo grows twice as quickly as the fastest growing tree, which makes it a very eco-friendly material. It is significantly harder and denser than other woods (such as maple) when compressed to the thickness required for a countertop, and it is sold in different swatches depending on how much space you need to cover.

Energy efficient lighting

Compact fluorescent lightbulbs

As stated on the ENERGY STAR website, qualified Compact Fluorescent Lightbulbs (CFL) use about 75 percent less energy than standard incandescent bulbs and last up to ten times longer. They also save approximately $30 or more in electricity costs over each bulb's lifetime and produce about 75 percent less heat. This makes them safer to operate, and they can reduce energy costs associated with home cooling. Any home improvement store should carry various sizes and shapes to fit in almost any fixture, for indoor and outdoor use.

LED lighting

Short for light-emitting diode, LED lighting systems use less energy than standard bulbs, which translates into a lower electric bill. LED lights are more expensive than conventional lightbulbs, but can pay for themselves over time.

Garage doors

Nothing dramatically changes tired curb appeal like a new garage door, especially if the garage is a primary focus of your home's design. It is best to have one that is a little different from the "contractor's special" found on every house in the neighborhood.

Return on Investment in Home Improvements

The following "Return on Investment in Home Improvements" chart is a summary of the results of HomeGain's national survey in 2007, based on the ten areas of home improvement identified by real estate agents in HomeGain's original survey in 2003.

HomeGain surveyed more than 2,000 real estate agents in each of the US regions. All agents might not necessarily agree on the same presale strategy. (See "% of Agents Recommending" column below.) Differences of opinions may vary based on the climate of the

Return on Investment in Home Improvements

Project	Typical Cost	Price Increase	Return on Investment	% of Agents Recommending
Lighten & brighten	$233 – 370	$1,178 – 1,566	355%	97%
Clean and de-clutter	$190 – 318	$1,505 – 1,937	578%	97%
Landscape front/backyards	$378 – 546	$1,718 – 2,158	319%	97%
Stage home for sale	$403 – 584	$1,938 – 2,431	343%	91%
Repair electrical or plumbing	$436 – 621	$1,205 – 1,590	164%	93%
Repair damaged flooring	$628 – 878	$1,633 – 2,061	145%	94%
Update kitchen & bathrooms	$1,404 – 1,828	$3,216 – 3,934	121%	87%
Replace or shampoo carpeting	$562 – 808	$1,532 – 1,950	154%	98%
Paint exterior walls	$663 – 938	$1,757 – 2,205	147%	88%
Paint interior walls	$651 – 920	$1,741 – 2,179	150%	97%

*Source: www.homegain.com

market, region of the country, or condition of the home in question. The percentage of agents that agree on the positive impact of a particular presale activity is summarized here.

According to a May 2007 survey of 4,000 real estate agents, 75 percent think that the kitchen is the most important place to make home improvements when selling a home. The Royal LePage House Staging Poll was also conducted by Maritz Research between January 26th and January 31st, 2006, and came up with the following percentages of buyers that would pay a premium for certain features:

Renovated kitchen	79%
Renovated bathroom	73%
New windows	70%
New flooring	62%
Updated decor	36%

In addition, while 47 percent of buyers said that the need for major renovations would most negatively influence their buying decision, another significant proportion of buyers (11 percent) thought that decor requiring major changes had the most impact on their decision. Only 6 percent of buyers said that the need for minor renovations would most negatively influence their buying decision.

CHAPTER 4

SET THE STAGE

Your property will need to meet specific requirements to be added to a list of homes that potential buyers want to view. Some of these concerns are fixed aspects that you cannot change, such as the location of your home, its number of bedrooms, the size of the house and property, its style, and particular features described in your marketing materials. However, how you address the aspects of the property that you can improve, including how you stage your home, will also contribute to whether or not your home ends up on such lists.

This chapter will provide you with proven tips and techniques for staging that apply to all areas of your property, specifically primary areas such as the front of the house and yard (how this area looks is referred to as "curb appeal"), the entranceway, the living room,

the kitchen, the master bedroom, and the bathrooms. It is essential for you to pay particular attention to these areas. They will make or break your chance of receiving an offer. The other areas of your property are still important, but usually will not discourage buyers from purchasing your house.

Developing a Staging Strategy

Your property identity and target market will guide your staging strategy. Therefore, you need to identify both before you can develop a strategy.

What is your property identity?

To know specifically how you should stage your house, you need to know what you are selling and to whom. To develop a profile of your target market, you need a clear idea of what you will be selling. This is your property identity. Write down the best features of your home to figure out the identity of your property:

- **Location:** Is your property in an urban, suburban, or rural setting? What are the local amenities? What levels of schools are in the area? What activities are in the neighborhood? Are there public transportation services available?

- **House elements:** Is it Victorian? Brand new? Old Century? Modern? Is it wheelchair accessible? Does it have one, two, or three levels?

- **Landscape:** Is your property a gardener's delight, professionally landscaped? Is the backyard completely or partially fenced? Is the backyard an open field or is it small?

- **Special features:** Is there a pool, hot tub, chef's kitchen, or large family room? Is the home energy efficient? Does it include energy efficient features, such as the furnace, air-conditioner, and lighting fixtures?

Who is your target market?

Now that you know your product identity, take into account the following variables to get an idea of who your potential buyers are. Write down your speculations as to what their needs are, and think about the following factors:

- **Demographic variables:** Age, gender, family size, family life cycle, education (primary, high school, secondary, college, university), income, occupation, socioeconomic status, religion

- **Psychographic variables:** Personality, life style, values, attitude

- **Behavioral variables:** Benefit sought, product end use, readiness-to-buy stage, decision-making unit, profitability, income status

- **Geographic variables:** Region of the world or country (east, west, south, north, central, coastal, mountainous), country size, city size (metropolitan cities, small cities, towns), density of area (urban, semi-urban, rural), climate (hot, cold, humid, rainy)

Examples: How to use your property identity and target market to create a staging strategy

Example 1

Property identity

You own a two-story home in a suburban neighborhood. There is an elementary school with playgrounds within walking distance. The property has a large fenced-in backyard and there is a mall nearby. Special features include a family room; a large eat-in kitchen; a walk-in closet in the master bedroom; and a master bathroom with a soaker tub, a separate shower, and a vanity with two sinks.

Target market identity

It is obvious that the best approach for this property is to stage it to attract families with young children. Typically, the age bracket for families with young children is getting a little older. You can safely assume the majority of your home buyers are going to be between 28 and 40 years old. The couple may not yet have children, but if they do they will tend to have an average of two children that are no older than 11 years old.

Staging strategy

The exterior of the home should be simple and virtually maintenance free, as buyers will not have a lot of time for property maintenance. Young families will respond positively to a spacious family or living room, a clean and organized large eat-in kitchen, and bedrooms set up to show how the space can be utilized for children. A master bedroom that provides a special hideaway will be well received, as will a luxurious bathroom.

Example 2

Property identity

You own a five-year-old, one level, three-bedroom home with a small backyard and basic landscaping. There is a small kitchen with a separate dining room and a patio door leading to a large deck. There is nothing extraordinary about the master bedroom and there are no added special features other than the separate walk-in shower in the main bathroom. The basement is a large room without windows. The house is in the city, on a bus route, and all amenities are within walking distance.

Target market identity

This home will appeal to many first-time home buyers, seniors, and young professionals. This scenario will attract the widest variety of people.

Staging strategy

This home should be prepared so that every detail has been attended to. This is the kind of house that especially needs to be pre-inspected. It should be decorated simply and staged primarily for entertaining. Stage the basement as a place to gather to watch movies, play poker, and entertain friends. Position furniture around a television — and no, size does not matter. All you need to do is create a simple media room. The dining room should be set for a family dinner and the deck should be staged for a small party.

Home Staging for Specific Areas

I've broken it up into primary and secondary areas. Use the checklists provided in Appendix III and on the CD to help you.

Primary areas

Once you have come up with a staging strategy, you can actually begin the staging process. The following sections detail what you should focus on in the primary areas of your home, which are the front yard and front exterior of the house (curb appeal), front entrance, the living room, kitchen, master bedroom, and master bathroom.

Curb appeal

The fact is that 78 percent of the decision-making process has already been made prior to arrival, based on the price and location of the house. Within seconds of seeing your home, potential buyers have formed an opinion of its overall condition and will likely spend the remaining time looking for consistency with the assumptions they made when they first viewed the home on the Internet. First impressions of the property's exterior should be "welcome home."

There is no transformation more effective than renewing the exterior of your house. Avoid turning potential buyers away with a less than desirable exterior. After all, they will be driving by before they call to request a viewing. You may have to fix and/or replace cracked or rotting materials, and you can also choose new colors for paint, siding, or trim. Again, make your house look different from and fresher than any other in the neighborhood, especially those that are also on the real estate market.

The key to curb appeal is balancing what makes you happy with what works in your community, since your home's yard, driveway, and exterior are both private and public spaces. Many magazines and newspapers often tout the financial benefits of boosting curb appeal:

- A 1999 Clemson University study showed that consumers valued well-landscaped homes at 11 percent more than the asking price.

- A Gallup survey, also from 1999, found landscaping could increase a home's value by 7 percent to 15 percent.

- In 2003, an article in *SmartMoney* magazine suggested that spending 5 percent of your home's value on landscaping could yield a return of 150 percent or more.

Take advantage of beautiful flowers and colors for ultimate curb appeal. Always use

A new black welcome mat and black urns with red flowers on both sides of the entrance door will definitely create a great first impression, whether or not you believe in Feng Shui. Add this to a freshly painted entrance door, new outside light fixtures, and a house number, and voila: a fresh new look that will tell buyers that this house is well taken care of. Be consistent with the house architecture though; don't use black urns for a contemporary house or stainless steel light fixtures on a Victorian façade.

Monica Stanciu
Staged 2 Sell Solutions Inc., ON

large pots or a group of three pots in different sizes for the best presentation. When you are selling it is not the time to skimp on flowers! Large arrangements look fantastic in photos and welcome potential buyers as they approach the front door. If space allows, add a chair and pillow that will make the space feel warm and inviting. Don't forget to add a simple but beautiful wreath to the front door. These little touches are what make potential buyers feel right at home.

Recommended upgrades: Exterior facelift and landscaping overhaul

- **Beautify the front door:** When dealing with curb appeal, the focal point is the front door. Upon arriving to the property, a person's eye should immediately locate the front entrance. Consider painting the door a different color than the others on the exterior of the house, or installing a unique door. Never underestimate the power of a red door; if your house style and color will accommodate red, do not be afraid to make the leap and use this color. Another way to spice up a door that is not "fancy," is to place a wreath or other accessory on it that will connect with the interior of the home. For example, if the house style is modern, place a modern piece on the door. Similarly, if the house style is colonial, place a traditional wreath on the door. Unless your screen door is new, you should consider removing it because they are often unsightly, noisy, and do not function as they should.

- **Install architectural details:** Installing large moldings around a front door will attract attention to it, especially if they are painted a contrasting color. This will add a little drama and charm to the exterior of the house and further increase its curb appeal.

- **Add shutters or accent trim:** Shutters are great for solving an architectural imbalance. There are some house designs that appear more dominating on one side than the other. By adding shutters to the weaker side, you can create balance. New composite materials, such as PVC resins or polyurethane, make trim details durable and low maintenance.

  Adding accent trim around windows and doors can create architectural interest to an otherwise boring exterior. It will add interest and separate your house from other similar homes in the neighborhood, allowing yours to stand out and attract buyers.

- **Update the "bling":** I believe that hardware is the jewelry on a house. Paying attention to these details can

---

Replacing the outside light fixtures, front door hardware, and doorbell can also make a big difference and impress buyers. Over time, these become worn and dated and can make a bad impression before buyers even step foot in the house. Taking care of these simple items is a small investment, but can have a large return and get you that offer!

Teresa Meyer ASP, IAHSP
Stage a Star Staging & Consulting Services, OH

create quite a significant impact. For example, if you saw a woman wearing a nice black suit but she was also wearing large, gold, chunky earrings from the '80s and a silver charm bracelet from the '70s, you might not think that she was well put together and you certainly wouldn't be impressed with her appearance. Now perhaps you saw this same woman in the same suit, but accessorized with discreet silver and diamond earrings, a silver neck chain, a silver tennis bracelet, and titanium diamond rings. She would likely make a significantly better impression on you. She would appear well put together, and you would be likely to assume that she takes care of herself and pays attention to details.

House numbers, lighting fixtures, kick plates, entry door lock sets, and wall-mounted mailboxes are all components of a stylish and attractive curb appeal. Choose all matching metals or colors and you cannot go wrong.

Update railings: Porch and deck railings can succumb to the effects of weather conditions pretty quickly if they are not maintained properly. If you need to replace any pieces before repainting, this may be a great opportunity to add character that can separate your home from others in the neighborhood. There are various options available, such as quality wood with various designs, PVC fencing, or wrought iron. As with other additions or improvements, ensure you choose color, style, design, and materials that coordinate with the home's main elements.

Refresh garden beds: Recreate the fresh garden look by weeding, pruning, and adding new mulch. This applies at any time of the year, especially during the winter when the "dead" look can take over a garden.

Keep up yard maintenance: Trim trees, prune shrubs, use a good lawn fertilizer and weed killer, and make sure the lawn is mowed and watered regularly. Keep in mind that lawns often go brown because they have been mowed too often and too short. Raise your mower's blade to allow the grass to shade itself and not burn out. This will also help to choke weeds and create a lush look.

If you have oversized evergreens and bushes that have grown to cover windows at the front of the house, trim them back to open up the view from the curb and to increase the amount of sunlight in interior rooms. Also trim bushes and trees to prevent obstructing walkways.

Renew your driveway: Your driveway is a welcome mat for your visitors. It should be a high priority on your list of repairs if it is cracked, stained, or has weeds growing through it. You do not have to invest in a completely new driveway, but renew it using the various products available. Make it look new by sealing a paved driveway, or by raking to level any displacement on a gravel driveway. You can even hire professionals to do these types of repairs with minimal investment, and you can include the receipt in your list of upgrades to give your real estate agent. The investment will probably equal the money and time you would spend doing the job yourself.

To further enhance your driveway, you can line it with stone, brick, or pavers. Lining is an increasingly popular upgrade, not only for its beauty, but also because it appears to widen the driveway.

Sell a lifestyle

Install window boxes: Add charm to the exterior of your house immediately with window boxes. They are easy to install and are available in a wide price range. Choose a color that is similar to your window trim or "jewelry," and that is in keeping with the style of the house. Copper and iron are materials used for a traditional look and painted wood provides a cottage feel. Choose plant and flower colors that coordinate well with the colors on the exterior of your house.

Establish new gardens: If you do not already have planting beds in the primary areas of your property, consider installing them — particularly along walkways and driveways, at the front corners of the yard, and immediately in front of the house. Include plants in various sizes and colors, and consider lining the garden beds with stone blocks or one of the other many materials available.

Add instant life: Create a colorful, lively welcome with container gardens. Place three or five container gardens in pots of various styles and sizes on the front deck. This is a particularly good idea for homes with asymmetrical entrances; for example, those with a window on only one side of the front door or that have a deck that's wider on one side of the door. Container gardens also look charming when placed symmetrically on both sides of stairs.

Use landscape lighting: There is something magical about landscape lighting. Consider installing low-voltage lighting for home buyers who drive by your home at night. Home improvement stores carry a wide assortment of affordable landscape lighting options that provide safety, security, and beauty. You can highlight unique features of the house, illuminate walkways for safe nighttime walking, and add accent lighting to large trees to create drama.

Include landscape art: Great landscaping makes for beautiful curb appeal and landscape art adds charm. Sculptures, water fountains, bird baths, and wood artistry are popular choices for a reason, but today's home improvement stores offer a wide variety of landscape art to complement the current home improvement trend: outdoor rooms. Select styles and functions that complement the home's exterior colors and elements. Consider installing a water feature; it adds relaxation and comfort to the ambiance of a well-landscaped property.

Enhance your landscaping: Arbors, garden gates, and decorative fence panels will also enhance your garden and the value of your property. These elements can be purchased at your local home improvement stores in easy-to-build kits or prefabricated sections that you simply connect together.

For optimum impact, paint or stain these items with colors that coordinate with your house.

- **Construct a pathway:** There is something special about walking on a garden pathway, as if it is an adventurous walk, like Dorothy's journey on the yellow brick road in the movie *The Wizard of Oz*. Installing a pathway around your property will add that magic both visually and in the experience it will provide.

    Adhere to the garden rule; there are no straight lines in nature, so build the pathway with curves. The materials you use should coordinate with the materials and style of what you have already chosen in your landscape plan. It doesn't have to be fancy or expensive. Crusher dust similar to what they use in parks is economical and natural. Patio stones, cement, brick — the possibilities are endless. Visit your local library if you do not already have a landscape book to see what suits your landscape and style of house. If you have an existing pathway, ensure that it can be walked on without the risk of tripping and pull out all weeds.

- **Reinvent your mailbox:** You can add charm to your home's curb appeal just by creating a unique mailbox that suits the house's style. You can replicate your home by painting the box the same color as your house and the post the same color as its trim, or you can use it as an address identifier by painting your house number on it with stencils (these can be found at your local home improvement store). I am partial to reflective numbers, as they are easier to see at night.

- **Take advantage of symmetry:** Symmetry is one of the simplest and most effective design techniques. Something as quick and easy as installing two matching lighting fixtures on either side of the front door will create a welcome and balanced entrance.

Clean, clean, clean

Cleanliness is essential for curb appeal; make sure that —

- doors and windows are clean;

- window frames are clean and clear of any moss or mold;

- light fixtures are clean and shine brighter;

- moss and/or debris from roof, gutters, and walkways, have been removed;

- all animal droppings have been picked up, even if you don't have a pet, as you never know who may have been in your yard in the middle of the night; and

- any litter that may have blown onto the property has been collected, especially anything that might be hidden in bushes.

Other tips and tricks

No matter what season it is, you should consider the following tips in order to make your house more pleasing to buyers:

- Choose exterior colors as follows: A primary color for the siding, a secondary color for accents (such as shutters), and a third color can be used minimally, usually for the front door. The rule of thumb is to never use more than three colors, unless your home is Victorian style.

- Take away any items that represent work, including home improvement materials or equipment. You want to sell a lifestyle to the emotional side of your buyer, meaning that you do not want to suggest the work that is required to maintain the property.

- Clear the front of any garbage cans, recycling bins, children's toys, bikes, and anything that was not planted (remember to remove weeds too).

- Remove any security company signs. It may give the impression that you need to scare thugs with the threat of security, or perhaps that the house has been broken into or is situated in a bad neighborhood.

- Remove any "Beware of Dog" signs.

- Park any vehicles in the garage if you are not already storing packed items there. Otherwise, park them away from the house or at the neighbor's.

- Clear away children's items and store them neatly behind the house or in a shed.

- If your house doesn't look like it's ready to be pictured in a magazine, take a look at it from across the street and see what you can do to make it more presentable.

- Open up your property by moving any boats, RVs, snowmobiles, watercraft, and ATVs to another location.

For winter viewings of your house, consider the following tips:

- Rake the lawn and garden beds to rid them of dead plants, leaves, and debris.

- Distribute fresh mulch throughout the garden beds.

- Ensure that the driveway and all walkways on the property have been cleared of snow and are safe.

- Look above the entrance for any accumulating snow or ice and remove it.

- Spread an ice melting product 30 minutes before viewings to ensure safe passage.

The following points will help you showcase your house during the holidays:

- Keep decorations simple and avoid any strong reference to religion.

- Cut evergreen branches and twigs to make effective, no-cost decorations for your outside pots. Complete the look with accessories (e.g., bows) and place some lights in the center of the pot.

- Keep holiday lighting to a minimum; festive, without trying to compete for a neighborhood prize.

The following points will help you showcase your home in the spring:

- Rake the lawn to freshen it after a long winter.

- Rake the garden beds to rid them of dead plants, leaves, and debris.

- Spread new mulch throughout all the garden beds to refresh them.

- Sprinkle grass seed and a really good fertilizer, and water your lawn well; it will be no time before your grass is lush and green.

- Plant annuals around the front door and/or porch area for an instant shot of color.

- Prune any shrubs or trees that did not get attention during the winter.

- Power wash the deck for a fresh new look.

- If your house has a front patio or porch, stage a social gathering. Spring is the time of year when people are looking forward to enjoying the outdoors, so this will encourage them to think positively when they enter the house.

For summer viewings, consider the following tips:

- Turn on the sprinklers for five minutes, a half hour before the open house. It makes the lawn and driveway sparkle.

- Rid gardens of weeds and rake to refresh the flower beds.

- Create clean lines when edging your lawn, and renew the look with regular cuts around walkways, flower beds, and driveways.

- Deadhead or remove spent annuals.

The following points will help you in the autumn season:

- Refrain from celebrating with decorations if you can. If holiday decorations are strongly desired, keep it simple; nothing is worth disappointing your children.

- Rake all fallen leaves to help rid the yard of a "dead" look and keep all walkways safe.

You can follow the "Curb Appeal Staging Checklist" provided in Appendix III and on the CD, to ensure that you've covered all of the bases during all seasons.

Front entrance

The front entrance of your home should be friendly, warm, and inviting, because it makes a very important first impression of the interior of the house. It will usually influence the viewer's entire perspective of the visit. If a potential buyer is left with a negative first impression of the interior, it is not unusual for him or her to focus on negative aspects of the home; however, a positive impression will influence him or her to focus on the positive aspects.

For the foyer, set a lamp in front of a mirror. The mirror will give the illusion of a larger space and will also magnify the light from the lamp. Foyers are the most important room in the house. If you do not capture the buyer's attention immediately, it will be an uphill battle.

Kathleen Lordbock
Re$ale Design & Home Staging, MN

Recommended upgrades: make a good first impression of the interior

▢ **Check on door hardware:** Upon entering the house, a potential buyer's very first impression of the actual house is the door handle and locking system. Make sure that the door hardware is working properly and smoothly. It is not a very good first impression if the key gets stuck and there is a struggle to get it out.

▢ **Be careful with area rugs:** Have you ever entered a house with several other people and tried to take your shoes off all while sharing the space? Now imagine doing this while trying to respect the home owner's property and stay on the area rug placed there. Potential buyers inevitably feel a need to remain on the rug with their shoes; it sets a mental barrier and can feel very awkward. Remove any area rugs or make sure that they are big enough for three or four people, especially for safety reasons during wet weather conditions. If there is sufficient room, make a place to sit available for those who have trouble putting shoes on while standing. It is also acceptable to post a sign that says "Please remove your shoes" to ensure that floors stay clean.

Sell a lifestyle

▢ **Keep furnishings and accessories to a minimum:** Aside from a small entrance table and a small space for someone to sit while taking off their shoes, remove all furniture to open the space and avoid hindering the traffic flow. If there is no drawer to hide "drop off" items, organize them in a decorative basket.

A sizable mirror in the entrance will reflect more light into the space; if possible, position it at 90 degrees to a window or a door with a window to maximize the amount of light entering the area. Window treatments are usually for decor purposes, so remove them to further maximize light.

▢ **Simplify the space:** Having a clear path and line of sight allows potential buyers to focus on space rather than where they are walking — so be sure to simplify the space. Clutter will close in a space and may cause a potential buyer to feel off balance or uncomfortable, especially in hallways and foyers. Imagine three or four people coming to view the home while you're still deciding what to keep and what to store. There needs to be room for them to take their shoes off without stumbling into one another.

▢ **Keep closets immaculate:** If there is a closet in the entrance, organize it and minimize its contents to only the items you will use every day. Ensure it is absolutely spotless and spacious. Hang coats on similar hangers arranged in the same direction and hide small items in baskets; order creates a sense of calm. This is usually the first door inside the house to be opened. It is a good sign if potential buyers are opening closet doors, as it means they are assessing whether the house will meet their storage space needs.

Be aware of the view: Also consider that up to five areas can often be seen from the front of the entrance, so it is important to make a big impact. Stand in the front doorway and assess which other areas of the house can be seen; keep these in mind when arranging furniture or choosing color in adjacent rooms.

Other tips and tricks

The sense of touch plays a big part in first impressions and can influence how potential buyers feel about a house. If you live where there are cold winter months, purchase three or four pairs of white, unisex, terrycloth slippers for potential buyers to use if the house has bare floors; it will encourage the feeling of a warm and cozy house. Also, ensure that the space is spotless, especially anything someone will touch, such as a door handle.

Consider built-in furniture to be a great investment. Some living rooms benefit from having shelving or cabinets built in beside the fireplace for added value and visual appeal. I had a client who had a fireplace in their living room that jutted out significantly and left spaces on either side where two tall bookcases looked perfect, like they were built-in. Unfortunately when they moved they took the bookcases with them, leaving the space looking like it was missing something. It looked very awkward.

Viewings will be short if the house is too hot or too cool. If it is a hot day and you have air-conditioning, turn it on. If it is cold, turn the heat to at least 72 degrees. The longer a buyer takes to view your home, the better the chance you have of receiving an offer.

The sense of smell also plays a large part in making good impressions. Make sure there are no odors! Negative smells such as rugs that smell like your pets, cooking odors, or the smell of smoke, will turn off many people and will negatively affect their opinion of the property immediately. Whether they are conscious of it or not, it will definitely focus buyers' attention on the negative aspects of the house, instead of the positive.

Smell can be a powerful influence. An increased number of people are experiencing allergies to perfumes, so refrain from burning scented candles to keep your house neutral and safe. Wash the floor with a pleasant smelling detergent (in scents such as orange or green apple) before every open house to welcome potential buyers with a very clean smelling home. This will give them the impression that the house is well cared for without knocking them over with a plug-in air freshener or spray. It might be helpful to have someone who doesn't live in the home determine if there are any odors hanging around. It is likely that you will not smell anything because you are used to it.

Ensure that all five of your viewer's senses have been considered and you will make a good impression. Above all else, make sure there are no odors. These can consist of cooking, baby, animal, smoke, perfume, or mildew smells, among others. There are buyers who will not go any further if there is a bad odor in the house; they will simply leave to view the next home instead.

Clean, clean, clean

Although there is less obvious cleaning to do in a foyer, make sure it still sparkles. Some things to check are that —

- floors, rugs, and windows are clean;
- the door is clean;

- any side table or closet shelves have been dusted; and

- the door and closet handles feel clean to the touch.

You can follow the "Front Entrance Staging Checklist" provided in Appendix III and on the CD to make sure you've covered all of the bases.

Living room

After the entranceway, the living room will usually be the second biggest influence on a potential buyer's reaction to the rest of the house. It is important that buyers feel at home in this room. You need to make this room special, especially if there is no family room in the house, as that means the living room will be where the family will spend most of their time together. Make sure that it is spacious and warm, and arrange the furniture in an intimate conversation area that still accommodates traffic flow.

Recommended upgrades: Enhance the room's "home" factor

- **Create warmth:** If your living room lacks warmth and charm, paint the walls a light, warm taupe. Check out the section "staging-safe paint colors" listed in Chapter 5 to help you decide which shade looks best with your room's trim. A limited number of neutral pillows placed on sofas or chairs can also add a warm look and feel to a living room.

- **Invest in added value:** Consider built-in furniture to be a great investment. Some living rooms would benefit from having shelving or cabinets built in beside the fireplace for added value and visual appeal.

Sell a lifestyle

A typical living room that is used as a family room will be cluttered and filled with a mixture of items from various individuals in the family. You know the room I'm talking about. A busy family that uses their living room usually creates a chaotic space. However, the living room is a perfect opportunity for you to influence a buyer to imagine themselves living in your home. Take advantage of this by removing clutter and creating a visual that implies a lifestyle suiting your target market.

- **Don't leave "footprints":** It is a natural human response to be distracted by collections, family photos, religious symbols, or other "footprints" that indicate that your family lives in the home. People unintentionally begin to develop a profile of who lives in the home and what type of people the home owners are, especially if your tastes are unique or not in keeping with viewers' tastes or opinions. The problem with this is that it usually disconnects viewers from the emotions needed to bond them to the home, which ultimately reduces your opportunity of receiving an offer.

- **Keep it simple:** Limit wall hangings to only one large picture or a smaller group of three pictures per wall, and remember that you do not need to have one on every wall. Create a nice visual by reducing items stored on bookshelves so you only use two-thirds of the shelves' potential space and organize items like an attractive store display.

- **Create warmth with a fireplace:** Rent an electric fireplace if the house does not have a "real" one or if you don't already own one. You can also use this as an opportunity to purchase one and take it to your next home, or you can leave it with the house and include it in the sale price. Using a fireplace as a focal point allows for a cozy furniture arrangement and can have considerable impact on the charm of a room.

Remove excess junk: Some people think a room needs to be filled with furniture and accessories to create a cozy environment. But in most cases, this makes a space feel closed-in and cluttered. A spacious room is also more desirable, so remove anything that is not used as part of a furniture arrangement, focal point, distraction, or strategy to manipulate traffic flow. Pack away all decor items except those intended for your display. A living room is typically used for entertainment and family time, so remove anything you wouldn't expect to find in a living room, such as a treadmill.

Keep toys out of sight: Anyone with children will surely understand the difficulty in keeping toys under control, but make an extra effort to keep them out of sight and in a storage unit that doesn't look like a toy box, or in a bin that can be concealed in or under a piece of furniture. Many people know what it is like to live with toys, but no one wants to trip over them in someone else's home. Besides, nothing creates a trashy look faster than a pile of colorful toys dominating the visual space of a room. Even if you don't have toys to contend with, it might still be beneficial to purchase bins to hide in or under furnishings, or a decorative sealed container placed on a side table to quickly clean up any clutter.

Clean, clean, clean

Make sure the room is immaculate before every showing. Be sure to —

- dust and clean all furniture (coffee tables, TV stands) and electronics (televisions, radios, stereos, computers);

- clean floors, walls, and windows;

- check that couches or chairs are clean and aren't harboring pet or other odors; and

- clean every detail of the fireplace or woodstove (if there is one in the

My tip is on staging the refrigerator. Buyers will inspect everything in the kitchen, and that includes appliances. Too often the refrigerator is overlooked and can become a haven for unpleasant sights and smells. If the refrigerator is a mess — covered in notes, magnets, sticky fingerprints, and dust-covered coils, and the inside has spills, old leftovers, and strong odors — it will turn off buyers and may affect how they feel about the rest of the home. After all, a place where food is kept should be clean. If that hasn't been cared for, what else hasn't been?

Pam Faulkner
Faulkner House Interior Redesign, VA

room), to give potential buyers peace of mind knowing that they will be buying a house that is safe. (Although it is normal to find a dirty fireplace or woodstove, cleaning it will indicate that your house is well maintainted and that you have taken the initiative to protect against potential fire hazards.)

You can follow the "Living Room Staging Checklist" provided in Appendix III and on the CD to ensure that you've covered all of the bases for your property.

Kitchen

The kitchen is by far the most important room of the house and it can make or break any sale. If your kitchen is not in line with today's trends, do your best to make it appealing enough to allow home buyers to envision its potential. It should be updated, stylish, spacious, practical, and absolutely spotless. Aside from aesthetics and function, you are also selling lifestyle in the kitchen. Removing everyday items from counters will prevent buyers from thinking about chores and enable them to imagine joyous events, such as holidays and having friends and family over for dinner.

If you have a kitchen that looks like it may need an update, some quick and inexpensive options are to change the hardware, install a backsplash, and update the flooring (ceramic is preferable but vinyl is fine). If you are selling a property at the entry level of your local market, a good cleaning should suffice.

Let's face it, most people don't want or cannot afford to replace a dated kitchen with a new one. Don't worry if you are unable to update all that your kitchen needs. Buyers just need to like the kitchen enough to see its potential. Much needed upgrades will be overlooked if you are offering an exceptional deal, or if the price reflects the kitchen's shortcomings.

However, you do need to invest in current upgrades if you are selling in a marketplace that demands a completely updated kitchen, which is usually the mid to upper portion of the real estate market in an area.

Recommended upgrades: Protect your list price with an up-to-date kitchen

- **Make affordable updates:** The quickest and most affordable way to make a huge impact in the kitchen is to replace cabinet pulls and knobs, the sink faucet, lighting fixtures, and flooring. If your countertops are dated, worn, or damaged, and need to be replaced, look into getting granite overlays cut and placed over existing countertops as an alternative to the popular expensive granite; they can cost one-third of the price! Otherwise, look at laminate as an option. There are some amazingly nice, natural stone imitations out there.

  Now is the time to decide if you want to take any items with you to your new home, such as lighting fixtures, fans, cabinet hardware, or plumbing fixtures. Replace them so you do not have to make any exclusion on your listing and risk having to negotiate with offers and counteroffers just to keep them.

Invest in flooring: The kitchen is one of the rooms where you will reap the most benefit by replacing the flooring if it is dated, worn, or damaged. A nice floor lends itself to cleanliness and style. Upgrading your flooring can improve your kitchen drastically. If you are confident that your house will sell within six months, take advantage of any "do not pay for six months" opportunities at your local home improvement store, and pay it off after your house sells.

Renew the cabinets: If your kitchen cabinets are too dated or worn, consider painting them a light cream color with melamine paint that will provide a solid, smooth surface. If you have the time and energy, take advantage of the opportunity to make a huge impact by adding an inside border made of small trim to the face of the cabinet doors; then prime and paint. This will add a little architectural detail and change the look dramatically. As tempting as painting cabinets may be, you may not want to attempt it unless you are experienced. It is difficult to ensure that it will look good if it isn't done by a professional.

Sell a lifestyle

Set the scene for a family gathering or party: People need to envision good times in a kitchen, such as holidays, social events, and family gatherings. So hide anything that resembles work and create a visual that suggests a family gathering or a party is about to take place. Everybody knows what a "real" lived-in kitchen looks like, but if you can create a visual that shows buyers what good times in the space will feel like, that will be what ultimately influences a buyer.

Clear it out: To accomplish this, it is necessary to keep all countertops clear of small appliances and other objects. If you cannot see yourself using an item within the next six to nine months, pack and store it away. Move appliances such as coffee makers, can openers, and toasters to a cabinet. Find a new home for reminders, receipts, Johnny's artwork, and family photos, and remove all "stuff" from the surface of the refrigerator. Minimize items kept on any surfaces, such as on a table or a window ledge. Remove everything from the top of all cupboards, such as display items or storage baskets.

Now put some back: A few charming pieces can remain, such as a small organized cookbook collection or neatly arranged cooking utensils. Display a fresh or good quality silk flower arrangement on the table and a bowl of fruit or interesting decor object on the counter for interest.

Clean out the cupboards: The idea of having strangers open your cabinet doors can be unsettling for some people, but keep in mind that it is a good sign. Potential buyers are giving serious consideration to the house if they need to find out if their belongings will fit in the new kitchen. Pack away everything in your cupboards that you do not expect to use within two weeks, including food, excess storage containers, and dishes used only for big gatherings. Give every cabinet and drawer a thorough cleaning and organize your belongings so they are neat and tidy.

Clean, clean, clean

The kitchen is one area that will highly benefit from plenty of time cleaning. Seeing someone else's mess can be a big turn off. Attending to the following details can really make your kitchen sparkle:

- Keep the sink clean and empty on a daily basis before leaving for work. The day you didn't will be the day there is a very interested potential buyer who wants to view your home right away.

- Clean and polish floors, any stainless steel, reflective surfaces, or tiles.

- Clean all glass, fixtures, faucets, and windows until they glisten.

- Clean all the hardware, especially cabinet doorknobs and drawer pulls. Anywhere a potential buyer is likely to touch is especially important. While seeing someone else's mess is a turn off, unexpectedly touching someone else's mess is a deal breaker.

- Give the cabinet doors a renewed look by cleaning their surfaces. I have always experienced success using Murphy's Soap to clean wood cabinets, and following it up with Murphy's Oil to give them a fresh new look.

- Wipe down all walls and baseboards; the Mr. Clean® Magic Eraser® is an amazing tool to take stubborn marks off the walls.

- An often overlooked detail is the backsplash. If it is tiled, make it look brand new by bleaching and re-applying sealer to the grout.

- Make sure your trash and compost bins are out of sight, regardless of where you store them for daily use. Also make sure that they are emptied daily and are odor free.

- Dust on top of your cupboards. When was the last time you saw the top of your cupboards? It will amaze you to know how quickly dust accumulates there! You never know when someone with dust allergies will walk through.

Other tips and tricks

- If you have a table in your kitchen and it is not round (which is ideal), create added space by reducing it to the smallest it can be. For example, if it has a leaf, remove it, or if it is a drop leaf table, drop the sides down.

- Before a showing, put cinnamon in a pleasant and plain kettle, boil it on the stove for a minute, and leave it for display. The smell of cinnamon is a non-invasive scent and will appeal to the majority of people.

- Avoid cooking anything that leaves a distinctive odor, such as fish, garlic, or cabbage at any time. You never know when you may get a potential buyer wanting to visit on short notice.

- An area rug is only recommended to minimize the presence of dated or unsightly flooring. It will not conceal a bad floor, but it will distract attention away from it so that it's not the first thing noticed when entering the room.

- Remove any added shelving or cabinets; they may give the impression that there is not enough storage space in the cupboards.

- Relocate or store anything you wouldn't normally find in a kitchen, such as school books, pet food, or medicines.

- When you have a showing, relocate the food, water dish, and anything else you have around for your pet.

- Put dish towels, dish cloths, and oven mitts out of sight. They are symbols of work, not decorating products, and shouldn't be used as such (even if they have ducks or flowers on them).

- For security purposes, store knives and other sharp objects high and out of sight. Not to frighten you, but I have heard some horror stories involving women in particular. You will want to eliminate any risk of harm, so protect yourself and your real estate agents from any worst case scenarios.

You can follow the "Kitchen Staging Checklist" provided in Appendix III and on the CD to ensure that you've covered all of the bases for your home.

Master bedroom

When assessing what to do with this room, keep in mind that the mortgage payers will be going to bed and waking up every day in this space, so the lifestyle it projects will influence their decision. Impress them with a simplified and serene space. This is a room worth a lot of effort and money, if you have any to invest.

Recommended upgrades: Create a luxurious space

The master bedroom is often neglected while decorating the rest of the house. If you are like the majority of home owners and you do not have a headboard, use pillows to create one. Stand two large pillows at the head of the bed in a color matching the bed cover and place two white pillows against the upright ones.

Create an even stronger focal point by centering the head of the bed on the far wall (from the point of view of someone standing in the doorway). Place a wall hanging above the bed that is three-quarters the size of the bed (or two or three smaller ones together to appear as if they are one large piece).

When preparing your property for sale, the master bedroom should receive special attention. To give it a mini facelift, why not buy new bedding and throw pillows? For approximately $200 to $300 you can give your bedroom that luxurious, hotel look that will help to get buyers' attention. The best part? You get to take it with you when you move to your new home!

Charlene Storozuk
Dezigner Digz, ON

Sell a lifestyle

If you create serene surroundings, you can appeal to a purchaser's desire for a serene lifestyle. By using luxurious fabrics, pillows arranged on the bed, and a monochromatic color scheme, you can evoke serenity, which is often sought after in a master bedroom.

A popular trend in the bedroom is a chandelier, as it usually lends itself to romance, which is appealing to most women and ultimately, most men. For an investment of about $75, it can make a huge impact on the look and feel of a room.

Decide whether to use window treatments

There is controversy surrounding window treatments. Some say they should be taken down altogether, because when selling a house you should be exposing the windows, expanding the room, and maximizing light. However, there are times when that idea just does not apply. I would recommend taking drapes down completely if you have a large master bedroom with extraordinary windows and/or views. But the majority of homes in subdivisions are relatively the same, and use similar standard windows. The room will need personality, charm, and warmth — which I believe can only be achieved with fabric and paint. There are also occasions when privacy is a concern and drapes are absolutely required.

That being said, drapes should not distract from any potential view, be an outdated style, or dominate a room. I am of the opinion that blinds have too much of an industrial look for a bedroom, so I recommend fabric drapes. Extend the curtain rod approximately 10 inches to 12 inches on either side of the window frame to allow drapes to open away from the window, maximizing daylight and the view.

Drapes should be a light neutral color so that the bed remains the focal point. Dark-colored or patterned drapes tend to throw the room off balance unless there is a tall, heavy piece of furniture on the opposite side of the room. This is generally discouraged so that you can keep the room open and airy.

Clean, clean, clean

A dirty bedroom does not suggest luxury or relaxation. Make sure that the room is immaculate before all showings and that —

- the bed is beautifully made;
- all laundry is tucked away in hampers;
- all clothing and belongings are put away in closets or dressers;
- floors, walls, and windows are clean; and
- all surfaces have been dusted.

Other tips and tricks

- Use a plain, light-colored bed cover to open the space. If you currently have a dark one that is light on the underside, turn it over for showings.
- If you have an extraordinarily large master bedroom and it does not require a new paint job, dress the room in a neutral color.
- Reduce the pieces of furniture to only the bed, two side tables, and one dresser (for an average-sized room).

- When you make the bed, allow for a lot of excess top sheet at the head of the bed. After placing the top cover on, turn the top sheet down over the bed cover and neatly drape over the side.

- Relocate books, Bibles, and magazines to a drawer, using only one or two items for display purposes.

- Remove anything you wouldn't normally find in a bedroom, such as exercise equipment.

You can follow the "Master Bedroom Staging Checklist" provided in Appendix III and on the CD to ensure that you've covered all of the bases for your home.

Master Bathroom

The best thing to remember about the master bathroom is that it is the place where your potential buyer will be getting ready for work every day. It should make him or her feel special and it should be a treat to spend time in. It is important to keep bathrooms absolutely spotless. This room should feel like a spa and there should be no evidence of anyone having used it.

Recommended Upgrades: Repair and replace fixtures

Replace or repair any outdated, broken, or stained fixtures. Although this may be an expensive endeavor, it could be worth your while if it will greatly affect your list price. If you are hoping to sell your home for a good price, you will not want to use sinks from the '60s or tubs with stains.

If your shower tiles, flooring, or countertops are outdated, cracked, or chipped, consider replacing them. These major features can also result in a good return on your investment.

If you are trying to sell a higher-end home and can afford to make the investment, consider installing energy-efficient appliances, such as a water-saving toilet. Another popular investment could be a walk-in shower.

Sell a lifestyle

It is important to arrange the bathroom in a way that shows off its best features. Keep the toilet seat down, pack away all personal items in baskets and place them under the sink, and display the shower and/or tub by opening the curtain or shower door one-third of the way.

- **Keep decor simple and fresh:** It is a good idea to display a set of luxurious white towels that you can use specifically for open houses or showings. Remove decorative bathroom rugs and covers; they hold moisture, can create an odor, and contribute to a dated look. You may want to use window coverings, if required, but remember that mildew can result from dampness and create an odor. It is also a good idea to display fresh flowers.

- **Eliminate clutter:** Do not display any personal items or reading material. Store anything you need to use on a daily basis in baskets, and place under the sink or in a cabinet. Pack any non-matching or extra towels, and put trash cans, cleaning products, or plungers under the sink or elsewhere out of view.

Clean, clean, clean

It is essential to keep the bathroom impeccably clean. Make sure that —

- there are absolutely no odors;
- walls and floors are clean;
- windows, mirrors, fixtures, and any other chrome, brass, or glass glisten;
- there are no signs of any stains, anywhere;
- there is no rust from the shower and/or tub and sinks;
- all countertops and surfaces are spotless;
- the grout appears like new; and
- the shower curtain or doors are clean and have no sign of soap residue.

You can follow the "Bathroom Staging Checklist" provided in Appendix III and on the CD to ensure that you've covered all of the bases for your home.

Secondary Areas

Although the following areas will require less attention when staging your home for sale, they could still use some staging techniques to further influence viewers to make an offer. These areas include the dining room, bedrooms, bathrooms, family or great room, office, rec room or games room, laundry room, basement, backyard, garage, hallways and stairways, and closets and linen space.

Dining room

The dining room is an important place to show lifestyle. Ensure that it is charming and warm, and that buyers are able to imagine their family and friends gathering there for dining, special occasions, and social time.

Recommended upgrades: Enhance the space

- **Lighting fixtures:** Once the house goes on the market you are obligated to sell everything that is screwed into the walls, floors, or ceilings. Before your real estate agent takes photos, take the opportunity to replace any lighting fixtures you wish to take to your next destination.

  If you are replacing a lighting fixture, you may want to upgrade to an impressive new one to make a statement. Ensure that you choose one that is to scale in the room and suitable for the style of your house.

- **Consider replacing the flooring:** If the flooring is dated, consider replacing it. If this isn't an option for you, you can also minimize the amount of attention a dated floor attracts by creating an accent wall that uses a color from the flooring, and painting the remainder of the room a safe color (see "staging-safe paint colors" in Chapter 5).

Sell a lifestyle

To sell a lifestyle to the viewer, it is a good idea to set the dining room table with attractive linen, dishes, and stemware to create a scene that he or she can imagine his or her family enjoying. For example, large families will want to know if big family dinners can be hosted in the dining room, so if you have a particularly large space, it would be a good idea to stage the room as though a large family will be coming for dinner.

Adding a fresh flower arrangement in the center of the table can create a particularly picturesque environment. You can also take advantage of space on top of a hutch by creating a small vignette with a bottle of wine, a few wine glasses, and a carafe (if available).

If room size is an issue, manipulate the space by using only four chairs around a dining room table instead of a typical seating arrangement of six. Remove any leaves from the table and relocate additional chairs to allow for more space. Rotate a rectangle or square table so that it is at an angle from the wall to make the room feel more spacious and maximize the flow of traffic. Generally, large pieces of furniture use a lot of visual space in a room. To open up the layout, keep anything that has heavy visual weight or is a dark color below 4.5 feet height. If you have a buffet and hutch and are using them to store items you do not use on a regular basis, pack and store the buffet and its contents. If the hutch is large and the dining room is small, store it.

If window treatments are necessary, they should not distract from any potential view, be outdated, or dominate a room; if they do, take them down to depersonalize the space, open up the room, and maximize sunlight.

Remove area rugs to expose nice floors, but keep them there if sunlight has lightened the exposed flooring (assuming you are unable to replace it). You aren't hiding anything, simply delaying the inevitable; until then you will allow potential buyers to fall in love with the house so they can overlook any flaws later.

Keep decor simple by minimizing wall hangings to just one or two pieces.

There are many homes in which home owners do not use a dining room as a dining room, but instead, use it for a different purpose (usually as an office). You will need to return the room back to its original purpose. Relocate anything that you wouldn't normally find in a dining room, such as a desk, computer, television, or workout gear.

Clean, clean, clean

The dining room is associated with food, so this room needs to be as immaculate as the kitchen. Ensure that the —

- walls and floors are clean,
- furniture is clean (food-stained seat covers, sticky messes left on the table, or food splatters on walls are a big turn-off and are red flags that scare away potential buyers),
- dishes on display are sparkling, and
- windows gleam.

You can follow the "Dining Room Staging Checklist" provided in Appendix III and on the CD to ensure that you've covered all of the bases for your house.

Bedrooms

Generally, bedrooms should be peaceful, clean, and tidy, and set up to look like bedrooms. Depending on your target market, there are several ways you could stage a bedroom. If it is not already used as a bedroom, convert it into a room you wouldn't necessarily use, but that would be of interest to your target market.

Recommended upgrades: Cleaning up

If the paint color in a bedroom is particularly personalized or outdated, or the walls are in bad shape, consider painting the walls a safe color (see a list of these colors in Chapter 5).

Like the walls, if the floors pose a particular problem, think about whether or not it would be worth it to replace them.

Sell a lifestyle

If a bedroom has been used for another purpose, such as an office or sewing room, it should be converted back. Many buyers are not able to imagine the room as it is intended to be used and may leave the tour thinking that the house had fewer bedrooms than they were looking for.

You can stage a room that suits your target market. There are a variety of rooms you may want to stage, depending on your property identity and your target market. The following are some ideas:

- **Nursery:** If your neighborhood has an elementary school and playgrounds, your property will be of interest to families who have young children or who will be having children within the next couple of years. In this case, it may be a good idea to stage a bedroom as a nursery; just make it peaceful, lovable, and gender neutral. These rooms are typically pastel colors, and it is best to restrict yourself to using soft greens and/or yellows.

- **Young child's bedroom:** In the same neighborhood, you could also stage a bedroom as a young child's room. It should be neutral, fun, and engaging. These rooms generally use primary colors. By using all three (red, blue, and yellow), you will make the room gender neutral while also evoking a fun atmosphere.

- **A pre-teen's bedroom:** If you live in an area with a middle school, fields for sports, ice rinks, or areas for other such activities, stage the bedroom as a pre-teen's room. This could involve a single bed nicely dressed using medium accessories, one or two posters on the wall above the bed as a focal point, and a few gender neutral toys (such as board games on the end of the bed or on top of a dresser).

- **Teenager's room:** If you live in an area with a high school, a mall, amenities, and areas for activities, stage the bedroom for a teenager. Include a double bed dressed in mature linen, a desk for a place to study, and a small dresser. Keep decorations gender neutral and accessorize so that the space is pleasant but serene. Include a few "props" such as books, school supplies, or a microscope.

- **Guest room:** If your property would be most appealing to young professionals (because it is located in the city and is not beneficial for family life), you can stage a bedroom as a guest room. This space should be luxurious, tranquil, and engaging. Include a double bed and dress it in nice linen. To distinguish this room as a guest room you can place a basket of bath products on top of a dresser and add a towel display consisting of a face cloth, a hand towel, and a bath towel, stacked neatly on one another.

You can follow the "Bedroom Staging Checklist" provided in Appendix III and on the CD to ensure that you've covered all of the bases for your home.

Bathrooms

The bathroom's influence on the purchase of a house has been decreasing; nonetheless, it is important that it is impeccably clean and fresh, and that it evokes a luxurious spa feeling. It should feel serene and luxurious, not display anything personal, and show no signs of personal use.

Recommended upgrades

The quickest way to update an outdated bathroom is to paint, change the top of the vanity and flooring, coordinate all hardware, and replace the sink faucet. If the tub is too damaged to spot paint, a cheaper alternative to installing a new one is to have it re-coated.

A current trend in bathrooms is soaker tubs and/or walk-in showers; if you have the resources, consider this a possible investment.

Sell a lifestyle

- **Create a "spa" look:** White, chrome, and glass can create a spa look and feeling. For example, you could display white towels, install chrome fixtures, and replace any door handles with glass knobs.

- **Use new towels:** Purchase white towels for display purposes only. Present them neatly over the towel bar, and fold a couple neatly and display them on the back of the toilet. Drape a bath towel over the side of the tub and remember to remove non-matching and/or extra towels when preparing for an open house or showings.

- **Keep it tasteful:** It is extremely important to keep the toilet seat down, as it is in poor taste to leave it up. Pack all personal things and store those you need daily in baskets under the sink or in a cabinet. Put trash cans, cleaning products, or plungers under the sink or elsewhere. Remove decorative bathroom rugs and covers; they hold moisture and can create an odor, and they contribute to a dated look.

- **Pay attention to the details:** Display a small bouquet of flowers if there is ample room on the vanity. Present the shower and/or tub by opening the curtain or shower doors one-third of the way. If there is no designated magazine rack, remove reading material.

Clean, clean, clean

The bathroom must be clean — spotlessly clean. Be sure that —

- all windows, mirrors, fixtures, chrome, and brass are glistening;

- any tile grout has been cleaned with bleach or been renewed with new sealant;

- any signs of stains or rust have been removed from the shower, tub, or sinks;

- the shower curtain or shower doors are clean and have no sign of soap residue; and

- fabrics such as rugs, curtains, and valances have been removed to minimize the risk of mildew odor.

You can follow the "Bathroom Staging Checklist" provided in Appendix III and on the CD to ensure that you've covered all of the bases for your house.

Family or great room

Use this space to help buyers imagine enjoying time with their loved ones playing games, watching television, or relaxing with a glass of wine and a good book.

You will appeal to many buyers if you invest in special features in the family room; ones that will help a family to enjoy the space more. If you have to replace carpet, consider replacing it with hardwood or laminate flooring, which is tough and can withstand a lot of the abuse animals and children can cause. Consider installing built-in furnishings such as cabinets or bookcases, or add charm to the room with a fireplace. The family room is very important and can have a significant influence on a potential buyer's decision.

Recommended upgrades

Installing a fireplace, new flooring, and built-in furniture in the family room are great investments if the existing elements are in need of repair or upgrades.

Sell a lifestyle

- **Remove all clutter:** Keep a decorative storage unit available for those last-minute showings; it is a quick way to clear a room of clutter. Store any furnishings not used for a specific purpose and put children's toys and games out of sight (unless a few are used to stage the room).

- **Keep decor simple and warm:** Arrange a limited number of neutral pillows to add a warm look and feel to the room. Install only one large picture per wall (or a smaller group of three).

Pack away all items, with the exception of a few for display, including two-thirds of everything stored on bookshelves. Display the remaining items in an organized and attractive fashion.

- **Create atmosphere:** As long as it is coordinated with other rooms, play soft music (if universal music is not available).

- **Consider removing window treatments:** It is always preferred that window treatments be removed to depersonalize the space, open up the room, and maximize sunlight; however, if privacy is an issue they can be used, but should not distract from any potential view, be outdated, or dominate a room.

Clean, clean, clean

Clean every detail of the fireplace or wood stove to show that the space has been taken care of and protected from potential fire hazards.

If there is carpet in the room, it would be wise to have it professionally cleaned. Chances are, it has endured many spills and can hold unpleasant odors if left untreated (especially if pets live in the home). For well-used family rooms, keep in mind that fabric furniture deserves a good cleaning too as it can also hold odors.

You can follow the "Family or Great Room Staging Checklist" provided in Appendix III and on the CD to ensure that you've covered all of the bases for your house.

Office

If there is an office or den in the house it should look and feel open, pleasing, practical, and organized. It is not usually a good idea to convert a bedroom into an office unless there are more than four bedrooms in the house.

Recommended upgrades

The office is a room where painting the walls a warm medium-to-dark color would enhance its attractiveness. Most office environments outside the home are bright, and most times, sterile. The opposite environment will be appealing to anyone looking specifically for a place to work at home.

Having the office prewired with a dedicated phone line would be a benefit in this room and having wireless internet installed would be a big bonus.

If you have an office in your house, you are likely to have more than two bedrooms in your house and will be attracting potential buyers who will be interested in having a nice office. Imagine one of those beautiful offices you see in magazines and try your best to apply some of the qualities such as a tree in the corner; books neatly displayed in a bookcase; desk lamp; organized computer desk; and inspirational artwork.

Sell a lifestyle

Be sure to put all personal information away and keep the top of the desk completely clear, with only a few items displayed. All electronics that are not used on a daily basis should be packed away and all electric cords must be neatly arranged. It can be a concern if a buyer sees a tangled mess of electrical wires. Remove two-thirds of all items from bookshelves and display remaining items in an organized and attractive manner. Don't forget to turn the computer off during all showings.

You can follow the "Office Staging Checklist" provided in Appendix III and on the CD to ensure that you've covered all of the bases for your home.

Clean, clean, clean

Use appropriate products for cleaning electronics, your LCD computer screen if you have one, and your desk; it shows you have respect if these items are well taken care of. Vacuum the floors and clean the windows.

Rec room or games room

A rec (recreation) room or games room is an added bonus, and tends to be in the basement. It is an extra room that can be used for leisure, a workshop, or a children's playroom; essentially, it is a place for fun. This area will not make or break the deal, but it is still safer to keep it tidy and free from obstruction.

Recommended upgrades

Recessed lighting is a great mood setter in a games room; create a party atmosphere with the room completely illuminated but kept dim.

To enhance the function of this space, install a surround sound stereo system if your target market includes families with young teens or older children and/or young professionals.

When there is an undefined area in a home (particularly in a basement) that has become the "landing strip" for unused exercise equipment, add more "space equity" by creating a home gym. For less than $100, that space can be transformed by adding a couple of full-length mirrors, bottled water, and rolled white towels. If the space has inadequate lighting, a small budget can allow for a new light fixture and a light paint color.

By defining this area, you will not only be adding "space equity," but will also be lending a "visual possibility" to prospective buyers to help them imagine living in the home themselves.

Teresa Mills-Schremm
Looking Fine by Redesign, OH

Sell a lifestyle

Let the games begin: Set up a table with a board game in progress positioned near a display of other board games set up on a bookcase, side or coffee table, etc. If you have a games console, set it up as though someone is playing it. For example, leave a few cartridges where they can be seen next to the console which is left out on the floor in front of the television.

It's a pool party: A rec room is just that, a recreational room where you go to play. If you have a pool table, set it up as though a new game is about to start. Take it one step further and set up an atmosphere of a pool tournament. If you have a score board, mark scores; set up a bar, turn on a stereo and use lighting to set a mood.

Child's play: If a child's playroom is staged, set the room up as though a child is playing and there are various areas of activity in progress. Just keep it neat and organized.

Reduce any items that do not help to create a simplified, showcased environment. Arrange furnishings to display a lifestyle of fun and leisure.

If you have a pool table, set it up as though a new game is about to start. If a child's playroom is staged, set the room up as though a child is playing and there are various areas of activity in progress. Just keep it neat and organized.

Clean, clean, clean

If there are windows, clean window panes and clear of them of any mold or mildew.

If you love pets, allow smoking, or enjoy whipping up delicious ethnic dishes, rent a commercial-grade ionizer to permanently eradicate odor with one flick of a switch. If you can smell it, you can't sell it.

Michelle Molinari
Feature This ... Certified Real Estate Staging and Interior, LA

This is generally one area that is last on the priority list for keeping clean but once it is clean, it is not likely you will have to go back to do it again any time soon. Make sure any glass items such as windows and mirrors are glistening, floors are clear of dust bunnies, and it's vacuumed.

You can follow the "Rec Room/Games Room Staging Checklist" provided in Appendix III and on the CD to ensure that you've covered all of the bases for your home.

Laundry room

Again, this room will not make or break a deal, but it can show that you love your home and take care of the details. Keep it clean, tidy, and organized. Do the laundry, place dirty laundry in the washer, or use a nice hamper to clear the area of any clothing or linens. Just make sure the area is cleared of all laundry and that the garbage bin is emptied. The area should be well lit to open up the space and to make buyers feel comfortable. Today's laundry rooms should be more than just a washer and dryer in a basement.

Recommended upgrades

Think green: If you sell a home in a middle price range for your market, consider including energy efficient appliances. People in this price range may not already own them and they might find it a very appealing feature in the home.

Create a work area: Ideally, a folding table and cabinets should already be installed but if not, consider it a good idea to do so. This room will not make or break a deal but it will be another one of those bonuses that will be fondly remembered.

Sell a lifestyle

Put it on display: It is advised to keep all laundry hidden for showings for typical laundry rooms with the exception of a laundry room with cabinets, a work table and areas to place baskets. It will help to sell a wonderful laundry area if you fold and stack various sizes of towels neatly on the work table and place laundry products neatly in appropriate places.

Create a workspace: If you do not have a laundry room and instead use an unfinished basement, arrange appliances to create a workspace that looks like a laundry room.

Store pet items: In homes with a cat, the laundry area typically houses the cat litter. Just before showings, store away any pet items, such as (freshly cleaned) litter boxes, cages, water dishes, and toys.

Never underestimate the power of staging outdoor patios, sundecks, BBQ areas, porches, etc. Outdoor living spaces are just as appealing to buyers as the indoors. Remove old, worn out, or rotted outdoor furniture and replace it with newer inexpensive pieces such as chairs, loungers, or tables. And don't forget to actually PUT PLANTS in all those empty pots that are simply filled with dry dirt.

Connie Tebyani
Platinum Home Staging, Inc., CA

Sometimes in the mix of getting [a] house staged for a quick sale we easily overlook the backyard. Outside patios are great selling points. Stage it as an extra sitting area. This adds square footage. Have a vase of fresh flowers, a pitcher of lemonade, and glasses to set the mood. This is icing on the cake.

Christina Rougerie, Divine Designing & Home Staging, LLC, TX

Remove clutter: Clear all items from any counter tops and place any excess supplies out of sight (including anything hanging on a line and the line itself).

Clean, clean, clean

Clean both the washer and dryer so that they look virtually new. Clean the lint tray to indicate that appliances have been well taken care of and are not a potential fire hazard.

You can follow the "Laundry Room Staging Checklist" provided in Appendix III and on the CD to ensure that you've covered all of the bases for your home.

Basement

Use a basement to showcase a simplified environment, and arrange furnishings to display a lifestyle of leisure. Also, make sure areas around walls and items of particular interest to home inspectors are free from any obstruction.

Recommended upgrades:

The basement is usually the last of investment considerations for home owners. If you have not yet had the opportunity, consider finishing the basement to add a considerable amount to the value of your property and increase its chance of selling faster.

The Total Living Area (TLA) consists of all areas of the property that are finished. There will be home buyers looking at this when qualifying properties to view, and if your basement is not finished the house will look smaller than it really is and it might be omitted from consideration.

Sell a lifestyle

Set the stage: If the basement is finished, find and arrange furnishings to reflect a lifestyle of leisure. If one is not already present, bring in a dehumidifier and/or an ozone machine to rid dampness and potential odors,

A stager can make our lives and that of the seller's so much better. I usually suggest that they clean and paint the garage. When they paint, they tend to remove everything not needed. This holds true with basements and laundry rooms as well.

Margaret Rome
The Real Estate Company of Maryland, MD

and turn on the heat in the winter months if applicable.

- **Remove clutter:** Store or pack any "when I get around to it" items and projects. Donate items that you no longer want or use, including sports or leisure items you haven't used in the last year. Organize any stored items neatly in one place. If there is a computer and desk in the basement, ensure that the computer area is clean and free of clutter and wires.

- **Life of leisure:** If the basement is finished, find and arrange furnishings to reflect a lifestyle of leisure suitable for your target market. This could include a home gym, home theatre, play room, or bar and kitchenette. If these are items you do not currently have, improvise with a few items just to make the suggestion of use. For example, a couple of dumbbells, a floor mat and a stability ball will suffice in making the suggestion of a home gym.

- **Remove smells:** To ensure your basement doesn't smell like, well, a basement, set up a dehumidifier to rid the space of dampness that breeds that musty odor. If there are other unidentifiable odors consider renting an ozone generator to eliminate any odors within hours.

Clean, clean, clean

Clean the fireplace or woodstove until it is immaculate and rid of any signs of mold or mildew. Clean furnaces, hot water heaters, and other appliances to appear as new as they can.

You can follow the "Basement Staging Checklist" provided in Appendix III and on the CD to ensure that you've covered all of the bases for your home.

Backyard

Professional landscaping is always a large bonus and a great selling feature, but a simplified, fresh yard that can reflect a lifestyle of fun is effective as well.

Recommended upgrades

- **Deck it out:** Every home should have a deck or patio at the back of the house to enjoy family barbeques, entertaining, and relaxing evenings under the moonlight. If you do not currently have a deck, consider it an important consideration. A traditional square wood deck would suffice, but also consider the popularity of stone patios stepped down to the ground.

- **Give it fire:** A popular feature of a backyard is an outdoor fireplace or fire pit. There are a variety of options for outdoor fireplaces at your local home improvement store, but consider a built-in version a considerable asset especially given concerns of fire safety.

Sell a lifestyle

- **Create an outdoor room:** Use outdoor furniture, a barbeque, and an outdoor fireplace (if you have one) to create a fun lifestyle with an outdoor room. This is a valuable extension of the house.

- **Remove clutter:** Neatly put away the garden hose, preferably on a hose reel. Return any gardening tools to the storage or garden shed. Dispose of any unused items, such as an old barbeque, broken chairs, or construction materials. Stash children's toys neatly in a designated area or pack them away in an outdoor storage box. Store any items that do not help create the setting of a simplified lifestyle.

- **Make windows sparkle:** Remove window screens to add a fresh look to the exterior of the house and clean the windows until they glisten.

- **Set up a fun backyard game:** Set up a net and leave a couple of rackets and a birdie next to it for a game of badminton, or a ball for volleyball. Or, set up a game of croquet or lawn bowling, whatever you think will be of interest to your target market.

Clean, clean, clean

- **All hands on deck:** Clear the deck of debris and consider a good deck washing a good investment of time, it may look brand new and you may not have to stain it. Clean the barbeque and fire pit to ensure any concern for fire safety is addressed.

You can follow the "Yard Staging Checklist" provided in Appendix III and on the CD to ensure that you've covered all of the bases for your home.

Garage

Ensure that potential buyers have the opportunity to drive their vehicle into the driveway so that they can imagine themselves coming home. If there are remaining vehicles left on the property, park them in the garage if you are not already storing packed items there. Otherwise, park them away from the house or at a neighbor's.

Keep garage doors down or closed at all times and keep the door into the house closed. Make sure the garage door opener is functioning properly.

Recommended upgrades

Fix any damage to the walls; a neglected garage can indicate that the home owner doesn't care about the house.

Install an automatic door opener if your garage does not already have one.

An attention getter for most home buyers is organized storage units and a work bench, both very good investments.

Sell a lifestyle

If you are like the majority of home owners and use your garage as a storage unit, take the opportunity to sort, pack, and store any items that are not being used on a daily basis. Organize seasonal items to be used within the next three months and store the rest (e.g., winter holiday or Thanksgiving decorations). Relocate any other items not usually stored in the garage, such as Aunt Susan's old tea cart that you promised to refinish one day.

Display tools and equipment neatly and store other items in containers on shelves for an organized appearance. Store garbage bins neatly and make sure that they are free of any odors; otherwise, consider relocating them to the outside.

Put insect sprays or anything to dispose of pests (such as mice or cockroaches) out of sight. Even if you've gotten rid of the problem and they are no longer on the premises, the products will scare potential buyers away. Carefully store any toxic supplies in plastic storage bins with lids and put them out of harm's way on high shelves. Take spent paint cans and/or other toxic containers to your local environmental depot.

Clean, clean, clean

In the garage, be sure to —

- 🏠 sweep and clean the floor;

- 🏠 paint the floor if its current paint is chipping, or if it has oil or chemical stains;

- 🏠 wipe away any spider webs and ensure that there are no telltale signs of insects of any kind; clean anywhere your potential buyers will be touching, such as a doorknob, railing, window, garage door opener, or light switch; and

- 🏠 clean the walls.

You can follow the "Garage Staging Checklist" provided in Appendix III and on the CD to ensure that you've covered all of the bases for your home.

Hallways and stairways

During an open house, it is important that buyers concentrate on viewing the house and not where they are walking. It is best to simplify the space, keep main traffic areas free of obstructions, and ensure nothing prevents easy passage.

Recommended upgrades

Anyone walking up the stairs usually does so while grabbing the banister. Change out the banister and the typical hardware with a slightly higher quality and unique design and it will make a considerable difference. Touch leaves a memorable impression, and walking up the stairs grabbing onto a smooth, solid banister inevitably makes it very noticeable, given most new constructed homes are built with minimum standards.

Sell a lifestyle

Make the space appear more open by not hanging anything on the walls, or by keeping them light in color. Remove all wall decorations with the exception of those on the far wall at the end (if you have a long hallway) and keep the hall completely clear of decoration if there is a closet at the end of it.

If you have a landing on your stairway, place an elegant piece of art in the corner, but

Organized closets and cabinets are a must when selling your home. Potential buyers will be opening and looking through them all to make sure there is enough space for everything. I tell my clients to make it look like Martha Stewart lives here. Use bins and baskets to put loose items in and create a simple, clean, organized look and feel to the space. Use matching fluffy towels folded neatly in the linen closet, and put a few scented dryer sheets between them. Going the extra mile with organization subconsciously tells potential buyers that the home owners have properly cared for and maintained the home. Visually showing organized spaces also delights the buyer, as they aspire to live that kind of life in your home.

Teresa Meyer ASP, IAHSP
Stage a Star Staging & Consulting Services, OH

not too large so as to impede the traffic flow. A nice tall, slim plant will also look very nice.

You can follow the "Hallways / Stairways Staging Checklist" provided in Appendix III and on the CD to ensure that you've covered all of the bases for your home.

Closets and linen space

As much as you do not want to hear it, buyers look in closets! Believe it or not, this is a good thing because it means that they are mentally moving in and assessing whether there is enough space for their family. Buyers will see that storage in the closets meets their needs if they are spacious and organized — so cut down on how many items are stored in the closet. If it is full to capacity, they will assume the closets are too small. This is a good opportunity to sort through items you haven't used within the past year and pack those items you do not use on a regular basis.

Recommended Upgrades

Install closet organizers. Storage is a priority for most home buyers and finding closet organizers in closets is definitely a memorable feature; it helps solve some of their problems.

Sell a lifestyle

Keep it neat. Hang clothes on wooden hangers or hangers that are all similar in style and color. Face them in the same direction for continuity and distribute clothing evenly and spaciously along the rod to give the impression that there is plenty of space.

For neatness and ease of use, store bedding inside its matching pillowcases and coordinate linens by color. Fold all items neatly and uniformly, similar to how you would find them in a department store. Organize small items you use daily in baskets placed on shelves. Keep floors clear of everything except neatly arranged footwear.

Clean, clean, clean

Even your closets need a good cleaning! Just as covered in the last section, keep your closets neat by hanging clothes on wooden hangers facing the same direction and organizing your linens. Distribute clothing evenly and spaciously along the rod to give the impression that there is plenty of space. Organize small items you use daily in baskets placed on shelves. Keep floors clear of everything except neatly arranged footwear.

Never underestimate the impact of a decluttered and orderly closet to potential buyers. Remove (and prepack for your eventual move) any out of season clothing and shoes, use matching hangers if possible, hang types of clothing together (i.e., tops, pants, dresses), face the hangers the same way, and pack all the extra closet "items" from the floor. Everyone appreciates a spacious closet, and by removing up to half of its current contents you highlight your home's available space. Let buyers relish the thought of filling your closet with their clothing, rather than having them want to quickly slam the door to escape the avalanche that may be your closet.

Tracie Burlage
Change and Arrange Interiors, VA

Be sure to —

- wipe down all shelving with a damp cloth;

- give interior walls, doors, and hardware a good cleaning; and

- vacuum.

You can follow the "Closets and Linen Space Staging Checklist" provided in Appendix III and on the CD to ensure that you've covered all of the bases for your home.

CHAPTER 5

MORE STAGING TIPS

The first and most difficult step is to detach emotionally from ownership; this is no longer your home. If you want to sell your house quickly, you need to look at it as a commodity, a product to be sold in the open market. You have to essentially become a retailer with a product to sell.

Incorporate the Senses

Keep in mind the following tips and techniques when walking through your house. Use the "Home Staging Checklists," available in Appendix III and on the CD-ROM, to work out a plan of action, as they can apply to every

One of the best tips I can offer sellers is for them to start emotionally detaching from their home when thinking of selling. Put on the eyes of the buyer and be very honest about how your house shows. From the baseboards to the cobwebs in the ceiling corners, personal collections, treasures, and wall color choices, you should scrutinize every little detail. Most people find this difficult to do and enlisting the help of a professional home stager or a trusted, honest friend can be just the spark you need to help you get on your way. Remember, your memories go with you — make your house a place where buyers can envision their memories beginning.

Karen Otto
Home Star Staging, Real Estate Staging & Consulting, TX

room. A general rule I follow when preparing a home to impress visitors is to satisfy as many senses as I can in each room. Use these tips as a guide to create a special experience.

Smell

There was a time when it was rare to hear of someone having allergic reactions to typical scents such as perfume, candles, incense, and air fresheners, but it has increased to a degree that it is best to avoid having these scents linger in your home during showings and open houses. A scent that will appeal to people with allergies and everyone else in general is the smell of freshness that comes with cleanliness. Just before a showing or open house, wipe all the floors with hot water and a mild cleaning solution. The smell of cookies or bread baking, or coffee brewing, makes it so obvious that you are working hard to impress. If you feel that it will work for your particular target market, go for it, but for experienced buyers it will only look like a phony act.

Touch

Buyers respond positively when they touch something that is velvety soft and plush. They cannot resist a blanket strewn over the end of a bed or the back of a chair, luscious bed linen and curtain fabrics, or extra plush white towels. Equally memorable (and not in a positive way) is when they touch something sticky or gooey on a banister, door handle, or cabinet pull. This is a big turn-off, so make sure that everything they may touch is clean.

Taste

If possible, leave a candy bowl or cookie jar available for people to help themselves. Leave a small, discreet card of thanks next to it that says something like, "Thank you for stopping by. Please treat yourself."

Hearing

If you are fortunate enough to have stereo speakers wired throughout your house, play background music that caters to your target market. If not, play music in the living room or family room. Currently, soft jazz seems to be the overall favorite genre.

Sight

Lighting

It is very important to consider lighting when preparing a room for staging. It will improve a potential buyer's ability to determine whether the space is large enough for his or her needs. It is important to illuminate all of the walls. If you cannot see a portion of a room due to a lack of lighting (such as a dark corner), a room may appear or feel smaller than it really is.

I encourage home owners to offer simple comforts to their "guests," such as bottled water or lemonade on ice in the kitchen or on the patio. Find out if interested buyers will be bringing children and set out sidewalk chalk, play dough, a small basket of toys, or clean snacks such as fruit snacks, boxes of raisins, etc. Occupying the children gives buyers a chance to really focus on the house and makes the children feel "at home" during their visit.

Shelley Roufs
StageRight, MN

Keep light natural

Use as much natural light as possible. This may require cutting back the overgrown bushes or pruning a tree around the exterior of the house. If appropriate, remove drapes to open the space and allow more sunlight into the room. If the drapes are in style, of good quality, and positioned so they do not interfere with the window, leave them up but keep them wide open.

Add your own lighting

Add extra lamps everywhere they look natural. Position a lamp on a table or place a floor lamp next to a chair. Every lamp needs to be anchored by a piece of furniture or it will look awkward and unnatural.

Try adding lighting to a real or artificial tree or large plant and place it in a dark corner. This could involve white tree lights or a spotlight inside a planter facing upward. This will provide a dramatic look and feel to the room. Also place a lamp in the far corner of a small room to draw the eye in and make the room appear larger.

Portable spotlights are small (five to six inches), inexpensive, easy to use, and versatile. They are great for giving additional light in a dark area or room, or for highlighting a piece of furniture by placing the light on the floor and shining it upward. Shine them at artwork or architecture and you have an instant art gallery. You can also place them behind a plant or screen to create drama and interesting shadows.

Types of lighting

- **General lighting:** Casts a comfortable level of brightness throughout a room. It is best achieved with a mix of sources, such as a central ceiling-mounted fixture and recessed spotlights around the perimeter. Dark-colored spaces need more general lighting than bright-colored rooms. To achieve adequate light levels using recessed can lights, install one every 20 to 25 square feet apart.

- **Task lighting:** Focuses on a specific spot, such as the baking center, and makes working much more comfortable. This type of lighting is best achieved with a mix of sources, such as ceiling- or wall-mounted fixtures augmented with under-cabinet lighting. Position light sources so the worker's shadow isn't cast on the work surface. Because of their high light-output and small size, compact fluorescent bulbs and halogen track lights work well for task lighting.

Lighting: You never know what time of day or night a potential buyer will drive by your house. Make sure the bulbs on your front porch, all outside entries, and the garage area are new. Stand in front of your house at night. Does your house have curb appeal even at night? Make sure all shrubs and trees are trimmed so as not to block any lighting, windows, or doorways. Lighting along a walkway is always a plus. Keeping your outside lights on while your house is on the market makes for an inviting look.

Liz Kennedy
Stage It Simple, TX

Accent lighting: Designed to spotlight a room's best features. It can be used to highlight a painting or to bring out the texture of a wall. Effects are best achieved with track lights, recessed lights, and wall-mounted fixtures — any beam that's stronger than the general lighting. Incorporate a dimmer to create a multitude of moods.

Bulb selector

Many sizes and styles of lightbulbs can be found at a good electrical supply store, but most fall into one of three categories:

Incandescent: Cast a warm, pleasant light and shows fabrics and paints in their true colors. However, these can make the room uncomfortably warm if too many are used.

Fluorescent: Compact versions that fit standard fixtures sell for more than incandescent bulbs, but use only one-third the electricity. For kitchens, use warm white (not cool white) tubes for best color rendition.

Tungsten-halogen: These low-voltage incandescent bulbs provide an intense beam that's ideal for spotlighting objects. They last longer and use less electricity than standard incandescent bulbs, but cost more up front and produce lots of heat.

Compact fluorescent lightbulbs (CFLs) are better than incandescent lightbulbs because they save lots of energy and are better for the environment; however, they tend to be dim. For the purpose of selling your home, change lightbulbs to incandescent bulbs with the most wattage for the fixture to maximize lighting in the space. This is also a good time to save yourself a few dollars by removing all your compact fluorescent lightbulbs so you can take them to your new home. It can be an expensive undertaking to replace them all at

---

Light fixtures should be appropriately sized and at the right height:

- **Bathroom vanities:** Lights should point downward to highlight the mirror's reflection (i.e., a woman's face when applying makeup).

- **Dining area chandeliers:** Chandeliers should point upwards so they are not shining down in people's eyes, and hang about 34 inches above the table top, centered over the table and not as the centre of the entire space. You should take into account that chairs will be placed around the table, and that will help determine the center point.

- **Can lights:** Should be spaced about 6 feet apart.

- **Ceiling fans:** For rooms up to 225 square feet (15 feet by 15 feet) and larger, use a fan with a blade span of 50, 52, 54, or 56 inches. In rooms up to 144 square feet (12 feet by 12 feet) I recommend fans with blade spans of 42 inches or 44 inches. Smaller rooms up to 64 square feet (8 feet by 8 feet) should use a fan with a 32-inch blade span.

Tori Ross
Ross Designs LLC, NE

once if your new home doesn't already have them.

How to use color

Color is a fabulous, versatile tool when preparing a house for sale. It can depersonalize, create a mood, add warmth, attract or distract attention, encourage the direction of the tour, and increase memory. All of this can be done with little money and time.

Depersonalize

A staging-safe color palette can depersonalize a space so the house will appeal to anyone who walks through it. Painting the walls with a neutral color palette will not offend anyone; there is something to be said for playing it safe. Remember, potential buyers do not have to love the wall color, but they have to like it enough to live with it until they can make the changes they want to personalize it. Until then, their personal belongings need to look good and the color of the walls cannot be an issue. This will not be the case for a house with interior colors from a dark color palette or rainbow colors. A potential buyer will refrain from putting in an offer simply because it looks like there is a lot of work to be done and money to be spent right away.

Mood

Color can set the mood in a room and make a person feel special, like in the master bedroom and bathroom. Home buyers paying the mortgage every month will be sleeping and getting ready for work every day in these rooms. If they feel great in these rooms, you've just increased their love for your home and your chance of receiving an offer.

Warmth

The use of color can allow people to feel more comfortable in a space that otherwise feels cold, such as a large open concept house or a bathroom that is fitted with all white fixtures.

Warm colors are based on yellows, yellow greens, oranges, orange reds, browns, and the like. Cool colors are based on blues, blue-based reds, blue-greens, greens, pinks, purples, and magentas. Once you have a basic understanding of warm and cool colors, you can then differentiate between, for example, a "warm green" and a "cool green." A warm green would be a yellowish green and a cool green would include more blue.

Using a warm neutral color will provide instant warmth to a room and will ultimately create a relaxed environment to encourage lingering. Remember, the longer a potential buyer stays in a room the increased chance they have of bonding with the house before they leave. Otherwise, it is a natural reaction for the majority of people to walk through rather quickly because they are not comfortable.

Attract or distract attention

The use of vibrant colors can attract attention to a particular highlight of a room, such as a fireplace, custom window, or architectural detail. Place a large piece of art above the fireplace that consists of reds, oranges, and/or yellows, and the eye is immediately drawn toward it upon entering the room (it becomes the focal point).

Vibrant color can also be used to distract the eye away from a less desirable aspect of the room, such as an old, outdated fireplace. Situate the living room sofa against a large wall and place the same piece of art on the wall above the sofa. Now the sofa becomes the focal point. Stage the room to display a desirable lifestyle and you've just minimized the importance of the fireplace to acquire a certain design or feel in the room.

Whatever color you choose to use as your attention getter, do not use it for any other purpose. Reserve that color only for attracting or distracting attention. Red is usually a good color for that. The other colors used in a room should be the chosen primary, secondary, and tertiary colors. Repeat a color in a room at least three times so it does not look like an accident.

Make your house memorable

Using color to highlight a special feature in your home will also increase the chances that potential buyers will remember your house over someone else's. The house will be remembered through reference to the attention getter, for example, "We loved the house with the bold painting above the fireplace. Remember? The room was so inviting and warm." If a picture is worth a thousand words, a picture with natural colors may be worth a million, memory-wise. Psychologists have documented that "living color" does more than appeal to the senses — it also boosts memory for scenes in the natural world.

Encourage the direction of a tour

If you want to manipulate the direction of a tour and how people view your home, place a vibrantly colored attention getter at or near the exit or entrance of the room you want them to move towards. For example, place a floor vase with a bright colored floral arrangement in the room you want people to walk towards and position it so it can be seen through the doorway. It will capture their attention and encourage them to move in that direction.

Use the power of bling!

I firmly believe that hardware is jewelry for the home; for example, cabinet hardware, sink faucets, lighting fixtures, and bathroom accessories. Consider what jewelry or accessories can do for a plain black suit. If you want to make a large impact on a room, change or update the room's "jewelry" and it will shine. Try to keep all your choices similar in metal type; for example, if you choose chrome in the kitchen use chrome throughout the house with the exception of the bathroom. A popular trend in the bathroom is still the "spa" look and feel. This can be accomplished with chrome, white, and glass. Use white for fabrics, such as towels. You could install chrome plumbing fixtures and towel bars, glass cabinet doorknobs, and a glass shower enclosure. Use the combination in various ways, however it pertains to your bathroom, and you cannot go wrong.

Decorating Basics
Painting
Types of paint to choose and why

If you have a typical situation in which you are painting walls that are virtually new, it is best to choose an eggshell or satin-based paint for its smooth appearance. If your walls have minimal defects, such as minor cracks, a messy spackling job, or uneven surfaces, use a flat-based paint to minimize the appearance of these flaws. It is always wise to ask for professional help from a paint advisor when you have extraordinary circumstances, such as bubbles under the surface, mold, or other oddities in the paint job.

If you are painting the walls of a home that was smoked in, you really need to wash the walls with trisodium phosphate (TSP) to remove nicotine before painting. Nicotine will seep through the paint and its smell will return.

Is it oil or latex?

Before going to the local home improvement store to purchase paint you need to know the type of paint that is already on the wall; you cannot paint latex over oil-based paint or vice versa. To find out for certain, dip a rag or cotton swab into denatured alcohol and rub it into the paint. If the paint comes off onto the rag, smears, or appears to melt, it's latex or another water-based product. If it remains solid, it is an alkyd or oil product.

Staging-safe paint colors

The list below is of staging-safe paint colors that coordinate with most decor. I have used the names from ICI Paint because ICI is available around the world. You can look for Dulux, CIL, Color Your World, Sherwin Williams, and Glidden in North America, but you are not limited to just these brands. If you have a particular favorite brand, take the name and paint number to your paint supplier, and they can usually make a match or translate paint codes to accommodate their brand.

As a general rule, use lighter neutral colors for all-over color and the darker colors to create accent walls or coordinate with a feature that cannot be changed. When choosing, consider the color of wood and other fixed items in the room, such as cabinets, flooring, bathroom fixtures, and drapes (if you choose not to take them down).

One time I staged a house that had vinyl flooring that would have been economical to replace, but instead I took a color from the flooring and chose to paint instead. It was even more economical and something I could do myself under the tight deadline I was working with. Then I created an accent wall in the dining room and painted the backsplash in the adjoining kitchen the same color to tie the two rooms together and coordinate with the floor. The rest of the space was painted ivory beige.

The following list includes staging-safe paint colors:

ICI Paint Colors

INDIAN PAINTING (A1739)	AUTUMNAL MOONGLOW (A0675)
IVORY BEIGE (A0661)	BEACHCOMBER (A1788)
LIGHT TAUPE (A1726)	BELLCOURT CASTLE (A0865)
MISTY GLEN (A0892)	BLUE SURF (A1451)
MOONLIGHT SONATA (A0149)	BURGUNDY (A0300)
MOONSCAPE (A0101)	COCONUT (A0834)
MUSHROOM CAP (A0739)	DAYDREAM (A0604)
NOSTALGIC TALE (A0605)	DEEP ONYX (A2015)
PEACH COLONNADE (A0722)	ELDORADO TAN (A0662)

RUSSIAN WHITE
(A0737)

FRENCH SILVER
(A1955)

SOFT KISS
(A0540)

GENTLE SPIRIT
(A0239)

STONE HARBOR
(A1775)

TUMBLEWEED
TRAIL (A1846)

TAFFY PULL
(A0576)

WEDDING WHITE
(A0071)

What to paint

If you decide to paint the entire interior, paint every room the same color to keep it simple. Your initial reaction may be that it will make your home "sterile" or "boring," but it will in fact enable buyers to view your home's features and not think about having to paint the walls because the existing color will clash with their belongings. It will also allow a seamless flow throughout the home and make the space feel larger than it really is.

Accent walls

If you find yourself dealing with a color in the room that cannot be changed (e.g., on the floor or counter), you can choose to paint one wall with this color as an accent wall. However, if it is an unattractive or dated color (such as dark green from the 1990s) and will dominate the room, it is best to avoid doing so. Choose a color that is two or three shades lighter or find another feature of the room to work with that will still coordinate with the "outdated" color.

"Must paint" areas

If you are limited for time, the spaces that must be neutral in color and looking their best are the entranceway, living room, kitchen, bathroom, and master bedroom.

Painting finishes

Painting unsightly and outdated finishes is a cost-effective alternative to completely replacing an offending finish. If you choose this route, it is imperative that you use a quality alkyd primer such as B-I-N or Prime-IT. If allergies are an issue, you may wish to use a super adherent latex acrylic primer such as Fresh Start (Benjamin Moore) or Gripper® (Glidden/ICI). Make sure you sand the surface before you begin.

Painting brick

Home owners often have difficulty with the idea of painting brick or wood. However, painting outdated brick on the exterior of a house can vastly improve curb appeal. It can be an effective way to update an interior space as well.

Painting a fireplace may seem intimidating, but it really is no different from painting anything else, such as a kitchen cabinet. If you paint it to match the trim in the room, you will play up architectural importance and create a nice focal point. You can also match it to the room's woodwork to emphasize its role as a natural focal point. If you prefer to minimize the impact of the fireplace in the room, choose a paint color that is a shade or two darker or lighter than the walls, and paint the mantel to match the trim.

If you are going to paint raw brick, get advice from a paint adviser at your local home improvement store for your particular project. A great tip that can save you a lot of work is to apply a good-quality exterior latex primer. It adheres to brick better than interior primers. Alternatively, you can also use a stain-blocking primer-sealer formulated for glossy surfaces.

To begin, brush on the primer and work it into all crevices. Then apply two coats of the desired color of latex paint (oil-based or alkyd paints are not recommended for brick, because they trap moisture). For the finish coats, a high-gloss or semigloss paint will show off the texture of the brick better than a flat finish and will be easier to clean.

Secrets of a great paint job

I have moved 19 times in 25 years and have had to paint every apartment or house I have lived in, both to create an environment that I felt good in and because I saw the value of a fresh coat of paint. When I first started out, I thought: "It looks easy enough — they do it on television. They paint a room in one day and it looks great so I can do it." Or so I thought! Over the years I've learned many lessons the hard way and picked up quite a few tips and professional painters' secrets to help you do a great job.

Get a bigger, more realistic swatch

The chips supplied by the paint company will help you decide what color family you want to choose from, but picking the actual color takes a bit more planning. The most effective way to find out if the final color you've chosen works with the size and lighting of the room you plan to paint, is to purchase a sample portion first. Paint two coats on a piece of white foamcore (purchased from your local office supply store — the white acts as primer) and hang it on the wall for a full 24 hours to see how the light hits it throughout the day. This is a great way to determine if the color you think you want is in fact as suitable as you had imagined.

This is a great technique if you need to choose between several colors you like or if you want to feel comfortable with a daring choice. Leave the foamcore up for a week and you will find that the final decision comes easily.

Know how many cans to buy

Start by measuring the surface area of the walls you'll be painting. If you are painting the whole room, measure the longest wall and multiply that number by the height. Then multiply the results by the number of walls. Take this number and multiply by two for two coats. For example: 12 feet (length) x 8 feet (height) = 96 feet x 4 (walls) = 384 feet x 2 (coats) = 768 square feet.

A rule of thumb for ordering is that one gallon will cover about 400 square feet. According to the previous example, you would be safe ordering two gallons to do the whole room because you've measured the largest space by four. It is always good to have a little left over for those inevitable scuffs and scratches that will need to be touched up.

Buy quality

Good quality paint will give you good quality results, period. The cheaper stuff looks great going on, but doesn't look as good when it is dry. In all likelihood, you'll have to paint more than two coats and there will be roller marks showing. This is especially true for darker colors. Save yourself time, energy, and money by purchasing good quality paint.

Prepare the area

Preparing the walls for painting sometimes means sanding, scraping, and making lots of dust. Remove as much as you can from the room before working and cover whatever remains with one-tenth of an inch (two to four millimeters) of plastic (it is reusable and it won't tear easily); tape down the plastic with painter's tape.

Give the walls a good scrub

We are all guilty of wanting to start painting as soon as possible to get the job done, but not cleaning the walls in some rooms can make the final product look awful. Grease, oil, and food residue can be an issue in the kitchen; and hairspray, shampoo, and other cosmetics can be a problem in the bathroom. These will prevent paint from adhering properly and in the end the paint job will be poor. Use a degreaser on tough areas and household cleaner elsewhere.

As mentioned earlier, nicotine on the walls from years of smoking in the home will seep through fresh paint and the smell of it will return. So do not think that painting over it will solve the problem. The only solution is to wash the walls down with TSP.

How to look for a good brush

There are plenty of cheap paintbrushes and I think I've bought them all. It wasn't until I borrowed a good brush that I truly realized the difference. Paint stays in the brush, doesn't leave lines, doesn't leave bristles behind, and doesn't have bristles sticking out the side after being used a couple of times.

A good brush should cost about $12 to $15. Look for a brush with bristles that are tapered, split, and assembled in various lengths to form a slim tip. If you plan to use latex paint, buy a synthetic brush (a polyester and nylon combination) because it will hold and release the paint really well. A paintbrush with natural bristles works really well with oil-based paints, but the bristles tend to swell and lose their shape when used with water-based paints. An unfinished handle will give you a better grip and prevent slipping, which is useful if you will be painting when it is hot; and stainless-steel ferrules are best because they won't rust after the brush has been washed.

You will also need to buy yourself a 2¼-inch angled sash brush for cutting in trim and a 3-inch brush for cutting in walls and ceilings.

Choosing a roller

Various sizes of rollers are available and should be used for different applications. The standard 9-inch roller cages and covers are great for painting regular-sized walls, but if you are painting a great room with high ceilings, you may want to consider the 14- or 18-inch rollers. They hold plenty of paint, which allows you to cover a larger area, faster. Small foam rollers are good for small areas, such as door panels and wainscoting.

Sandpaper

Foam sanding sponges covered with black sandpaper then coated with silicon carbide are truly the best tool to prepare anything for painting. They can be used wet or dry for different applications, they won't clog as frequently, they are flexible enough to get into the tightest of areas, and they can bend for curved areas. Best of all, they are reusable. Standard brown sandpaper works well enough, but clogs are more frequent so it won't last as long.

Use fine grit (200 or 220) sandpaper for smoothing surfaces between coats of paint, medium grit (100 or 120) when prepping walls that are already in good shape, and a coarser 60 or 80 grit to take the edges off paint that is chipped or peeled.

Taping tips

Painter's tape is sold in blue or green and should be used when you are unsure of your ability to paint without making a mess. The tape is barely tacky so it will stick and lift off without taking anything with it (unless you leave it on for a long period of time).

After you've taped the area you want to protect from paint (such as the corner where the wall meets the ceiling or trim), run your finger along the edge firmly to press the tape hard into the wall. This will give the tape a good bond and decrease the chance of having paint bleed under it.

If you do not remove the painter's tape as soon as you are finished painting, be sure to score the line between the tape and the trim with a blade. Latex tends to be a little rubbery when not dried completely and it's likely that some of the paint will peel away when the tape gets pulled.

Paint wet on wet

When painting a room, there are two jobs that run simultaneously if you want a professional finish. One is cutting in and the other is rolling. Always cut in first, which means painting about 1½ inches in from the edge. While the paint is still wet, then fill in the rest of the wall with a roller. This will help you to avoid creating a "band" that tends to show around the edges where there was cutting in. It can be very obvious where the cut-in paint was allowed to dry before the rest was rolled

on. Many people do not realize the importance of painting wet on wet. If you are working alone, cut in only as far as you can roll before the paint dries.

Keep it smooth

The following tips will help you to keep your final coat of paint smooth:

- **Lint:** To obtain a professional finish you must keep lint from getting onto the freshly painted walls. Before you dip the roller into the paint tray, take a roll of tape and wrap it backwards around your hand so that the sticky side is facing outwards. Pat down the entire roll several times to pick up any little stray hairs and lint.

- **Chips of paint:** When you are dipping the roller into the tray, try to avoid putting it in so far that the paint touches the roller arm. Not only will it drip and make a mess, but if you store it for later use without washing it off, the next time you use it you'll find little pieces of paint have chipped off and landed in your paint and on the walls and you will have a nasty time trying to get rid of them.

- **Dust:** It would be wise to wipe the walls to rid them of dust, as paint will apply poorly if there is dust. Use a Swiffer®, microfiber dusting cloth, or cheesecloth to wipe the walls before rolling on the paint.

In what order should you paint?

Multitasking is a great way to get several things done at the same time, but it doesn't work to your advantage when painting. If you need to paint the walls, the ceiling, and the trim in the same room, stick to doing one area at a time to obtain sharp lines (they will be compromised if you try to do them all at once). Paint the trim first and the ceiling second so you don't have to worry if the paint spills onto the wall. After they have dried, cut in the wall and roll on the paint right away (again, paint wet on wet).

Cutting in line

Cutting in is the term used to distribute paint along a straight line where the wall and ceiling (or trim) meet. To cut in on a wall, load your brush and spread the paint onto the wall working the brush up to the line between the wall and ceiling. Flex the brush and glide it along the edge, watching where the paint is going and how much is being distributed. Left-handed people should do this from right to left and right-handed people should start left and move right to maintain a maximum view. Do not over reach, it will only risk messing up a clean line and is not worth the extra foot in coverage. If you have really good hand-eye coordination, watch where you want the paint to go and hold your hand steady, and you'll get a clean, straight line. Like how you hit the ball in baseball, keep your eye on the ball and follow through.

If you are painting the baseboards, go ahead and use painter's tape on the floor. Just be sure to tuck a small portion of the tape under the baseboard to ensure you do not create a paint line where it meets the floor. If you are using painter's tape on carpet, put the tape as far under the baseboard as you can and run your finger across the tape pressing down so that you are tucking the carpet fibers out of the way as you go. This way, any paint that may get onto the carpet fibers will be hidden when the tape is removed and the fibers move back to their original positions.

Windows take too long to tape. If painting around them, overlap the glass by $\frac{1}{16}$ of an inch to seal the wood. Then, after the window is dry, scrape excess paint off the panes with a straight blade.

Through thick and thin

When you are rolling on the paint, pay attention to how thick you are applying it. Coverage is important, but so is the consistency and texture. Make sure you apply the same amount of paint on all of the walls during each coat. Avoid pushing on the roller and you'll avoid splatters, and hold the roller evenly against the wall to prevent ridges from forming.

Once you've finished rolling a section of the wall, go back and make several long vertical strokes from the top right to the bottom of the wall in one motion. This last step will spread the wet paint evenly across the surface.

How to load a brush

Assuming you've purchased a good brush, paint will move up towards the top of the brush and the metal ferrule. To prevent overloading your brush, avoid dipping it into the paint more than halfway. Then tap the bristle ends against both sides of the paint can to remove any excess.

Keep it clean

If you accidently drip water-based paint onto the carpet, do not scrub it. Instead, blot the area with a dry cloth and then with a wet cloth. If you spill a lot, blot as much as you can, keep the area wet with a wet cloth, and call a carpet cleaning company. A professional should be able to clean the area completely.

To clean up spills on non-carpeted areas, my all-time favorite gizmo for quick spills or splatters is a baby wipe. It's moist enough to wipe away any paint residue and dry enough to not leave the area wet.

Immediately after painting, thoroughly clean your brush with a mild soap and water and make sure that you've rid the brush of paint close to its core or metal ferrule. Run a metal brush comb through the bristles under running water if you happen to have one; if not, continuously run your fingers through the bristles until the water runs clear. Squeeze the brush to remove excess water and blot the bristles dry with a soft absorbent cloth. Return the brush to the original package to maintain its shape for the next time you want to use it.

Various painting tips

Do doors right

Painting a door in place works okay, but I recommend that you remove it to ensure you get professional results — especially for a front entrance door. This is the first impression of the entrance to the home, which is where expectations are set. A messy paint job is disappointing to see. Remove the hardware, lay the door on a sawhorse, and paint in long, vertical strokes, and while the paint is still wet, lightly brush over the surface to level out the finish. Wait until the paint dries completely before painting the other side and rehanging.

Forgo daily cleaning

There is no need to clean your brushes and rollers if you are going to continue painting the following day. Simply wrap them in plastic, squeeze out any air, and place them in the refrigerator or freezer; latex paint dries slowly in cold temperatures. Just remember to allow the roller to return to room temperature before reusing it.

Expect touch-ups

Accidents always happen; inevitably, someone always enters the room and touches the wall. Keep a cheap sponge brush on hand to blend a patch with the rest of the wall or woodwork. To mimic the look of a roller, simply dab on the paint.

Bleeding paint

Apply a thin, feathery coat of paint along the line where the tape meets the wall and let it dry before you paint properly. This will create a proper bond to protect the paint from bleeding under the tape. When you are ready to take the tape off, carefully pull and you will find a clean line with no bleeding.

If you are handy with a caulking gun, run a small bead of caulk along the line where the painter's tape meets the area to be painted. Use your finger to thin it out as much as possible, then remove the tape. The thin bead will create a seal better than any tape. This is a particularly good technique if you are painting stripes. After a few hours, peel off the caulk.

Caulk all cracks

Filling gaps with a paintable acrylic-latex caulk cuts down on drafts and makes your trim look better than new. The secret to using caulk well is to cut the tip smaller than you think it should be; too much caulk makes a mess. Also, instead of using a nail to break the inner seal, use a small wire so you do not stretch out the nozzle. Consider buying a dripless caulk gun, which will automatically back off the pressure after each pull on the trigger to prevent unwanted oozing.

Finish what you start

Do not start a wall unless you are committed to finishing it right away. Do not break for lunch, go to the washroom, or answer the phone. If the paint is not of a similar consistency, depending on the color choice, a line may show up where wet paint overlapped onto dry paint.

Space layout and furniture arrangement

When determining how to lay out a space and arrange furniture, consider the following tips:

- Plan your arrangement on graph paper first to save yourself from moving furniture several times. Use the "Furniture Layout Grid" (available in Appendix I and on the CD) to help you.

- The size of furniture pieces relative to one another and to the size of the space is called scale. For the purpose of staging, you'll want to have as many pieces that are similar in scale as possible, to create a harmonious atmosphere.

- When furnishings are in various sizes that do not belong together (e.g., a too-small rug under a rather large piece of furniture), it can make the space feel "off" or uncomfortable.

- Large or tall pieces can close in a room just by affecting peripheral vision, so keep as many pieces below 4 feet high/wide as possible. Also keep as many dark pieces out of a small room as possible; it is the color weight that will again, close in a room. If you have to work with dark furnishings, cover them with light-colored covers and keep them small.

- Make sure that all the tall or heavy pieces do not end up in the same area of the room; it will throw off the room's balance.

- If you are working with various-sized pieces, mix small- and large-scale furnishings by grouping small items to balance with one large piece. For example, two small chairs and a small side table grouped together across from a large sofa.

- Create strong focal points in all rooms. When entering a room, take an objective look at the space and determine the focal point. This could be a unique window, a fireplace, or a beautiful piece of furniture. Whatever it is, be sure it is something you want your potential buyer to focus on. It should call attention to the special features of the room and highlight why potential buyers should purchase your home over someone else's.

- After determining the focal point, place large pieces first when arranging furniture.

- Consider how you want the buyer to move through the space when arranging furnishings. For example, if your windows are not in the best shape and you cannot get them replaced, place a large piece of furniture in front of them to prevent a direct sight line onto the windows. Place these furnishings first, and then work from there. You are not hiding anything, but rather delaying the inevitable upon home inspection.

- Be sure that viewers can move through the space freely without having to watch where they are walking. You want them to pay attention to the highlighted features in the room, not the flooring. Primary traffic paths need a minimum of 24 inches of space so people can move through comfortably.

- Try angling one or two pieces of furniture slightly and moving furniture 4 to 6 inches from the wall to create more interesting room spaces.

- Arrange and stage a room for its intended use. If you currently use a dining room as an office, remove its furnishings and set the room up as a dining room.

- If you think staging a room as a nursery (or other specific room) would target most interested buyers, remove current furnishings and set up the new room, even if you have to borrow or rent items. This will help potential buyers to imagine themselves in the house.

- When you think you are finished, stand at the entrance to the room and evaluate if the color weight is balanced. It will feel very awkward if there are too many heavy colors or there is just one color on one side of the room.

Cozy ideas for large spaces

It can be quite an undertaking to create a room that is inviting, comfortable, and fashionable, especially in a large or open-concept space. Consider how you feel when you walk into the room. How a room looks is virtually irrelevant; it is how it makes you feel that will make a world of difference. Grouping furniture in an intimate setting will ultimately create the cozy feeling you should be aiming for when staging a home for sale. When considering furniture arrangement, comfort should be your end goal. If the pieces in a room don't work well together it really doesn't matter how nice your furniture is — it will feel uncomfortable.

Here are some ideas you can use to make your large rooms seem more cozy and comfortable:

- Creating more than one or two furniture groupings is an effective way to make a large room cozy. For example, a great room might have a grouping

There are not very many items you can add to a room that have as much impact as an area rug. They add color and texture and create a space within a space. They can also be layered over carpet to detract from existing dated carpet. Look for rugs with two or three colors at the most and avoid busy patterns. And remember, the area rugs go with you when you move!

Elaine Manes
A Wonderful Space LLC, CO

in front of the large window over-looking the lake, and another grouping around the fireplace set up for a relaxed evening with great conversation and a glass of wine. Likewise, an oversized kitchen may have a cooking area, an eating area, and a lounging area for entertaining guests as you are cooking.

- If you are trying to decide what to do with an oversized room, such as an open-concept room in the basement (which is common), it is best to establish multiple-purpose rooms that can be divided into zones. For example, in one room you can have a home office, a family room, and an arts and crafts area.

- If dividing spaces is your goal, you can use an area rug that is close to the scale of a furniture arrangement to create the feel of a separate room. The rug will anchor furniture pieces together and will help to define the room or grouping in a large space.

- Just as light neutral colors make a small room seem larger by reflecting light, dark rich colors absorb light and make the room seem smaller, something you can consider for an oversized room that you need to make feel cozy.

- If you have very high ceilings in a large room, you can visually lower the ceiling by painting it darker than the wall color.

- Moving the furniture away from the walls will reduce floor space and will make the room feel intimate.

- Using built-in furniture will add value to your home and use extra space. You can add an entertainment center or built-in shelves or storage around the fireplace. You can also create a cozy place to read next to library shelving.

- Adding plants and accessories is a quick and inexpensive way to make a room inviting. Because many small knickknacks and smaller plants and flowers will look like clutter in a large room, place items in the room that are suitable for its size. Large plants and accessories for large rooms.

- It is true that oversized furniture will take more space both physically and visually, but you will need to avoid outfitting the entire room in oversized furniture. Having too many big pieces will make you feel very small and overwhelmed.

- Wall art should be scaled with the size of the room. Tapestries are a great and creative way to fill the wall with oversized art in a large open concept space.

Hanging pictures

Follow these tips to use pictures to enhance the look of your home:

- Hang pictures at the center point of the average eye level, approximately 4 feet and 5 inches the floor if viewed from a standing position, or 3 inches to 6 inches above a piece of furniture (from the bottom of a frame) if it will be viewed from a sitting position.

- In the dining room and living room, pictures should be hung so that they are at eye level when viewed from a sitting position.

- All pictures in the room should be relative to one another. They should be hung with similar measurements from the top, bottom, or middle.

Area rugs

It is usually recommended that you should remove area rugs; however, there are occasions where they are useful:

- To create a cozy sitting arrangement in a large room. The rug should be large enough to extend under all the furnishings, but should stay 2 feet away from any walls.

- To tame a dominant floor. A light colored rug can take care of this.

- To distract attention away from a damaged floor. You aren't hiding anything, because it will be picked up during a home inspection.

Cleaning and Simple Home Improvement Tips

To make the most of your decorating, you will need to take care of basic cleaning and home improvements. Here are some tips to do this well:

- Blend a cap full of vanilla with acrylic paint to make the smell milder.

- Artist-quality paints sold through art supply stores come in many fabulous colors, including metallic colors to touch up picture frames or to enhance a plain frame or mirror. The tube paints (rather than the liquid paints) are concentrated and you can rub them into the surface of a dull or chipped item to give it a fresh new look.

- Painting unsightly or outdated finishes is a cost-effective alternative to completely replacing them. It is imperative that you use a quality alkyd primer such as B-I-N or Prime-IT first. If allergies are an issue, you may wish to use a super-adherent latex acrylic primer such as Fresh Start (Benjamin Moore) or Gripper® (Glidden/ICI). Make sure you also sand any surfaces before beginning a project. For longer lasting durability, use alkyd paint to finish.

- If you are finished painting for the day but you are not yet finished the project, wrap the wet paintbrush in plastic and put it in the freezer. The next day when you are ready to paint again, take the brush out of the freezer and let it thaw for five to ten minutes before continuing to use it.

Use framed wallpaper or fabric as art. It is a quick and easy way to [create] unique, inexpensive art. I keep numerous frame sizes on hand and paint them to match the decor. You can also use them as mats for black and white photos or other items.

Beth Baker
Beth Baker Interiors, PA

- White toothpaste is a quick and easy way to fill nail or hook holes in the wall or ceiling; a very simple repair.

- Scrub surfaces with a lemon (cut in half) to get rid of scum and limescale on bathroom fixtures and drains.

- An inexpensive way to clean the interior glass on a wood burning stove is to dip a damp paper towel in the ash inside and rub it on the glass.

- Use peanut butter or vegetable oil to remove black marks on floors.

- To remove watermarks on wood furniture, mix one tablespoon of lemon essence or oil with two tablespoons of rubbing alcohol. Rub into the mark, then buff with a soft cloth.

- To clean silver, put tin foil in the sink (shiny side up). Place your silver items on top and pour boiling water combined with half a cup of baking soda on top.

- Complete minor repairs and focus on the upgrades that matter the most, such as light and bathroom fixtures, and flooring.

And the final, but most important tip:

- Bring in another pair of eyes, preferably a professional stager for a consultation. This person may see problems you've missed. The majority of people live with problem areas as long as they don't see them.

Remember, Love Is in the Details

Don't be intimidated if you aren't comfortable with your ability to decorate a room and have never really considered the importance of strategic placement of your keepsakes and possessions. To obtain a look like those you see in magazines and make a room more "charming," go to a furniture store and get an idea of the details used to beautify the living room or bedroom. Stores that sell furniture tend to do a wonderful job putting a room together. It is their job to sell you a lifestyle that will influence your decision to buy their furnishings, similar to your objective with staging your house. Take a look at how they position furniture to capture the ambience and how they place accessories such as groupings, pictures, and objets d'art appealingly on bookcases, other pieces of furniture, or walls. Or look through some decorating magazines for ideas; there are various issues at your local library so you do not have to spend a fortune. The following are some tips to help you along:

- When displaying groupings such as candles or books on a table, consider the rule of three:

If you have shiny brass switch plates or knobs that you want to change the color of without painting, try Easy-Off oven cleaner. It essentially tarnishes the brass, lending it a blackened look somewhat similar to that of rubbed bronze. I did this in a dining room I staged with a rustic Tuscan look and it turned out beautifully!

Sharon Roark
Home Stager & Realtor, RE/MAX PREMIER, KY

1. Less than three can look too sparse,

2. More than three borders on clutter,

3. Use varying heights to make the grouping interesting.

A fireplace adds charm and a welcoming, cozy atmosphere at any time of the year. If you have a working fireplace that generates heat, light a fire for showings during the fall and winter. During spring and summer months, place a lit grouping of large candles into the insert. If you have a fireplace used for ambiance that does not create any heat, turn it on for all showings.

Remove valuables, prescription medicine, and breakables. There will be various types of people walking throughout your home, particularly during open houses. A person cannot be everywhere all the time during a showing. You or your real estate agent will never know for sure what a visitor's intent is when he or she is viewing the home.

If you sell your car, it is always recommended that you detail it before the sales manager at a dealership views it so he or she will offer you a better price. The same rule applies to selling your house. If you do not have the time, hire a professional service to clean the details of your house, including carpets and windows. It is surprising what you do not see when you live with it. When was the last time you saw the back of your bathroom cabinet?

Arrange fresh or silk flowers throughout the home. Constantly having fresh flowers in the home while waiting for viewings isn't very realistic, and silk flowers have come a long way from the once popular plastic variety back in the '70s. Often you cannot tell the difference between real flowers and good-quality silk flowers. However, if you are selling a higher-end property, it would be wise to invest in beautiful displays of fresh flowers for open houses for that added "wow" factor.

Clear out closets and clutter. This is where pre-packing will benefit you in many ways. The house will feel more spacious, and having the majority of your items packed will make you less stressed when you have sold the house and are on a deadline to move. It is best to store boxes and furnishings off site, although buyers are forgiving of storage boxes neatly tucked away in a garage or basement.

De-personalize the home by removing photos, mementos, dated items, and intimate valuables, such as weapons or religious items. Protecting these

Don't forget small details like a name on a mailbox or a door knocker, and don't forget the house numbers. When buyers are looking to buy a home they don't want to see the home owner's name on the front door ... it makes them feel like they are intruding on their space.

Stacey Holt
Setting the Stage, AL

should be a priority, so if these items cannot be temporarily stored away, move them to an area that can be enclosed (such as an armoire). Home buyers generally do not open personal furnishings, but they will open closets and anything that is being sold with the home.

- Put away large collections — porcelains, plates, and so on. Not only are these items personal, but buyers may get distracted by the collection and overlook features in the room you want them to see. Another benefit to pre-packing your collections is that it can protect them from potential damage or theft.

- If you want to add color to a room that lacks style and time is limited, paint only the wall that you see when entering the room in a color that has a punch and coordinates with the furnishings and accessories, but is still staging safe.

- Use pots or inexpensive wicker baskets to fill in empty spaces. Use them to display a plant or hide items you use daily but do not want buyers to see.

- To give a small room the appearance and feeling of a much bigger room, install a mirror in a bold, pretty frame. If you can, position it 90 degrees from a window (to reflect light into the room) and you'll open up the space even more.

- If you decide to keep your drapes, install curtain rods approximately 6 inches to 12 inches outside the window frame so that when you open them it will allow maximum sunlight into the room and brighten it, causing the room to feel larger.

- A mirror above the fireplace is usually a nice idea, but unless it reflects a good view or adds depth to the room, choose a large wall hanging instead. For whichever one you choose, make sure that it is large enough to be the exact size or a little smaller than the length of the fireplace.

- If you need to fill a vacant bedroom or convert an office back into a bedroom, purchase or borrow an airbed if you do not have access to a spare bed. I have even heard of other stagers using boxes to create the look of a bed. After it was made up, people could barely tell the difference. The point is the suggestion; that is really all you need to accomplish.

- When you leave the house for an expected showing of your property, make sure you leave your driveway open so buyers can drive their vehicles into it and imagine themselves coming home.

- There are some areas and seasons that will bring insects into the home whether or not you are the best housekeeper. To avoid the chance of scaring away any offers, consider calling in an exterminator to protect your home from uninvited visitors.

- Anyone who loves their pet finds it difficult to believe someone would not be pleased about having them around — after all, he or she is adorable and harmless, right? But, please do not take the chance. Not all buyers will appreciate your pets. Many people are allergic or afraid of various pets, so arrange for your pets to stay somewhere else for all showings and tuck away all of their supplies (such as water, food dishes, and litter boxes).

- For quick and easy cleanup in the morning before leaving for work or to prepare for last-minute showings, use storage bins that are either decorative, or shaped so they can be hidden under or in a piece of furniture.

- An economical way to dress up a plain, square bathroom mirror, is to create a frame by using decorative molding glued around the perimeter. Measure and cut molding on 45-degree angles and paint it to give the impression of an expensive mirror.

- If your home has 2-inch baseboards, create an illusion of 4- to 5-inch baseboards by installing small molding approximately two inches above the existing baseboards. Paint the molding and the two-inch portion of the wall all one color. To create the illusion of a higher ceiling, paint the entire wall and baseboard the same color.

- If you have an unpleasant view and do not want to lose sunlight with drapes to hide it, apply vinyl window frosting and smooth out the bubbles with a credit card. If you wish to allow in more light, use a utility knife and carve out small shapes such as stars.

Little red flags

After moving into our homes, there are many ways in which we make them more comfortable for our day-to-day living. When you put your house on the market you may not be aware of seemingly harmless little details that will be red flags for potential buyers. These little red flags will subconsciously influence buyers' judgment of how the house meets their needs. Some of these indicators are as follows:

- Many small repairs that are easy to fix can imply that the house was not loved and therefore not well cared for.

- Extra storage units or cabinets in the kitchen or in the bathroom, particularly over the toilet, will suggest that there isn't enough storage space.

- Linen, towels, and blankets found anywhere other than in a designated linen closet indicates that the house does not have a large enough linen closet.

- Strong scents, such as a room deodorizer, candles, or incense, can imply that you are trying to cover up something.

- Large security company signs in your windows or yard will suggest that the house is located in a bad neighborhood or that your house has been broken into.

- Insect or rodent repellents found easily in a closet, or stored openly in the garage or shed, will suggest that there is an infestation.

- A plunger that can be easily found within reach of a bathroom can be a sign of possible plumbing problems.

- Normal-sized bedrooms that are large enough for a typical family can appear much smaller than they really are just by having too much stuff in them; this clutter can make potential buyers walk away from your home thinking the bedrooms are too small.

- A four-bedroom house that uses one bedroom as an office or craft room will be remembered as a three-bedroom house.

- A "Beware of Dog" sign will discourage anyone who is afraid of dogs or has allergies from viewing the house, even though you may have taken Fido somewhere else and had the house professionally cleaned.

- Undesirable items, such as old lumber, car parts, or broken things scattered throughout the property, implies a lack of pride in home ownership. Assumptions will be made that the house is not well cared for.

- To veteran home owners, a few harmless cracks in a brand new house are normal because of settling, but they will alarm first time home buyers and may discourage them from being interested in your house.

Don't Forget Curb Appeal

Nothing sets a good mood like color, and approaching a house with great curb appeal will set your potential buyers with the right outlook when viewing your property. The following tips are for those of you who have limited experience gardening and are intimidated with the prospect of deciding what to plant where.

Basic gardening

Ten steps to a new garden bed

1. Clear out an area for your flowers. The best location for curb appeal is on either side of the front door, where potential buyers will enter the home.

2. Consider a kidney shape for your garden; it will always looks more appealing when it is curved and not square.

3. If you have to remove grass, use a sharp tool to cut and shovel out the loose grass.

4. Lay down landscaping fabric or newspaper to cover the entire surface of the garden.

5. Spread a layer of soil throughout the entire flower bed and compact it; just walking over it evenly should do the trick.

6. Spread another layer of soil so the garden is approximately two inches higher than the grass or surrounding area. (The soil will settle after a few rainy days.)

7. Take the flowers that you chose and position them on the garden bed after referring to the growth specs on the tags. Place higher growing plants towards the back and keep shorter plants in the front. Mix the colors throughout.

8. Dig holes that are the depths recommended on the flower tags and plant your flowers.

9. Water flowers generously using a watering can or a gentle setting on the hose.

10. Spread small-sized mulch throughout the garden.

Purchasing flowers

Before heading to the gardening center, take measurements of the garden beds you plan to fill and determine if they are in areas that have all-day sun, half-day sun, or are primarily shaded.

Go to your local gardening center and ask someone to help you buy plants that suit your needs. Give the person the size of your garden and the amount of light it receives. If you are left on your own to determine what to buy, do not fear. On each plant you will find a tag that tells you the name of the plant, the size it grows, the amount of light it will tolerate, and when it blooms.

To keep it simple, choose flowers that are white and flowers that are a color that compliments your house. When choosing your plants, keep an eye on their height; you do not want to have all tall plants or all short plants. Remember that you want to put tall plants in the back of your garden, medium-height plants in the middle, and low-growing plants in the front.

Other products required

Purchase soil that has the appropriate nutrients for your plants. This is not the time to learn how to develop proper soil conditions for various plants and bushes. A garden-center employee can help you with this, but there is usually a general soil mixture that would be appropriate for most popular choices.

Also remember to pick up landscaping fabric, which will prevent weeds from destroying your efforts (newspaper is a great short-term solution and an alternative to landscaping fabric) and mulch (small-sized mulch for flower gardens and medium for trees and shrubs).

Landscaping with mulch

A garden bed lined with mulch improves the garden's appearance, protects the plants' root systems, slows erosion of topsoil, and adds much-needed nutrients to the soil. Though applying mulch may seem like a lot of work, it can actually save time later in the season because mulch helps prevent weeds and retain moisture. Not that you plan to stay, because you are selling your home! But if you do remain there for a while, you will not need to bother much with maintenance.

Things to remember when applying mulch:

- A 1- to 2-inch layer of fine mulch should be sufficient, while a coarser material should be 3- to 4-inches deep. Too much of either can suffocate your plants. In areas where you want to stop anything from growing, lay it on as thick as you like.

- Coverage will vary greatly based on what type of mulch you use and how deeply it is layered.

- Do not put mulch down too early in the spring, as you need to give the soil a chance to warm. Normally, mid to late spring is the best time to put down mulch.

- The area needs to be free from weeds before mulching.

- Water plants before applying mulch.

- Pull mulch 1- to 2-inches away from woody stems and tree trunks to prevent stems and bark from rotting.

- The chunkier the mulch you use, the deeper you need to make the layer. Fine mulch tends to work its way into the soil quicker.

- Seedlings can grow through a thin layer of mulch, but if the layer is too deep it can be too difficult; therefore, let your plants get off to a good start before you add mulch. You can always add more after the plants are established.

- Mulch that is too deep will stimulate root growth in the mulch layer rather than in the ground. The resulting shallow-root system is susceptible to cold and drought damage.

- Consider scale when deciding what mulch to purchase. Large pine bark nuggets will be too large for a bed of annuals but perfect for an area around trees or shrubs.

- Consider a heavier or larger mulch for pathways, slopes, and areas prone to flooding or high winds.

- You may need to apply additional mulch in the summer to retain moisture and in the winter to insulate from the cold.

- If your garden has a layer of winter mulch, pull it away gradually as the temperatures warms. If you remove it all at once, the tender new growth underneath could be affected by a late-season cold snap.

- If you wish, you can work most organic mulches into the soil at season's end to improve the soil.

Pruning

Pruning is essential when plants, trees, or bushes look untidy, dominate the space, intrude on traffic areas, or prevent sunlight from entering the house. If you have a professionally landscaped property, it would be wise to hire someone to do your pruning.

There are various strategies behind landscaping and a specialized knowledge in pruning numerous types of plants, trees, and bushes is required. Generally speaking, the best time to prune is early spring and late fall.

There are four basic pruning cuts, each aimed at producing a different effect:

1. **Pinching:** Simply pinch off a terminal bud with your thumb and forefinger. Typically used to prune annual and perennial flowers, and some vegetables.

2. **Heading:** This cut is used to prune farther back on the shoot than you would for pinching. With handheld pruners, cut right above the leaf where the lateral bud has already grown.

3. **Shearing:** Use handheld or electric hedge shears to create a hedge or a bush with spherical or square form.

4. **Thinning:** Use handheld pruners, loppers, or a pruning saw to make thinning cuts depending on the thickness of the branch being cut. Each cut removes an entire stem or branch, either back to its point of origin on the

main stem or to the point where it joins another branch.

The following are some basic pruning tips:

- Use scissor-cut hand shears for precise cuts on branches up to ½-inch thick.

- Use long-handled loppers for the extra leverage needed to cut branches up to 1¾ inches.

- Use a bow saw to cut large limbs quickly.

- Make a cut just above a growth bud at 45 degrees, with the lowest point of the cut opposite and even with the bud.

Decluttering and Storage Solutions

Without a doubt, there are plenty of storage solutions to help organize your home life. What you may not realize is that getting rid of or organizing clutter can also beautify your home. For example, a room without clutter will appear larger and more inviting. In addition, some of the available storage solutions can be decorative furniture pieces. Of course, the home storage solutions you choose will depend on the types of items you want to store and the frequency with which you need to retrieve them.

Before you begin, you need to assess your ability to be realistic about what you need, what you want, and what you cannot let go of. This is your opportunity to determine what you really need to keep and what you really need to store. We're all guilty of buying larger houses or storage solutions to accommodate more "stuff." Most people haven't even had the chance to go through it all to find out what they actually have! There is likely plenty of stuff they may not even need or want any longer. Belongings just seem to multiply by themselves!

Seriously, the days of collecting and displaying trinkets are gone — and thankfully so. The weekly dusting alone would take up any limited time you may have for yourself, if you are lucky to have any at all.

Furnishings you've kept 'just because'

I too battle with the temptation to keep things that I "may" need in the future. But in the vast majority of cases, the items have simply wound up gathering dust and taking up space. So here's your first task before you select home storage solutions for your items: Go from room to room, including the closets, garage, attic, and basement, and pull out all of those items that you are holding onto for

This is a no-brainer, but it's surprising how often it's overlooked. Take down those cute little collections that you love. They mean something to you, but buyers may think of these as clutter and they won't see the great features of your home. This includes bookshelves, wall collections, counters, pass-throughs and more. Then, arrange the furniture so there is a single, clear focal point in each room. Remember, we want to show off your home, not your furnishings!

Debbie Fiskum
Perfect Transformations, CO

no good reason. My rule of thumb is that if you do not foresee wearing it or using it within the next 12 months, then seriously consider giving it to someone who would make use of it. Obviously, this notion excludes important papers and key reference materials (e.g., warranties or instruction manuals).

All is not lost, however. You can earn money from your discarded items by having a yard sale. Or, you can simply make a charitable donation to a nonprofit organization, such as a church or a shelter. Be sure to get a receipt so that you can deduct the value of the items on your next income tax return!

Once you've eliminated the things you do not need, consider these home storage solutions for the items that you want to keep:

Furniture

- **Armoire:** You can find armoires in many styles and storage configurations. They will add beauty and presence to any room. In general, I would recommend using an oversized armoire for storage rather than two smaller pieces of furniture. From an interior decorating perspective, your room will appear much bolder and more interesting.

- **Chest of drawers:** If you need to separate items by type, then a chest of drawers would be a good choice. For example, storing all of your Tupperware containers and respective lids, or tea towels and kitchen hand towels. As with an armoire, I recommend that you get one that is large, with deep drawers.

- **Storage chests or trunks:** These items are good for storing bulky items such as quilts and blankets. Of course, you can use them to store toys, books, or just about anything else. Many decorative trunks can also double as various types of tables (i.e., coffee tables or end tables).

Closet organizers

- **Closet storage:** Many home improvement stores offer closet organizer options. Consider investing in a design that best suits your current needs and can change and expand to accommodate future needs.

Shelves

- **Pre-built shelves:** The benefit of shelves is that you can use them to take advantage of a wall's vertical space. Many shelves are quite decorative and can be used to store or display personal items and collectibles. This option also adds value to the home, as buyers are always looking for storage solutions.

I use "event bags"; I love a staged linen closet. Use Space Bags for events, such as what you would want to use, wear, sit on, etc., for the Fourth of July, or early fall clothing for the family, or saving this for my sister's family pile. Label them properly and stack them together so they can be easily accessed in the near future, but are out of sight.

Sheron Cardin
how2homestage.com, CA

Bookcases: A custom-built bookcase can be used to make a statement and be the focal point of a room. However, there are also many quality assemble-it-yourself options, which are not too daunting for even an amateur. Bookcases are not just for books, they can also be used to store sheets, towels, and other linens.

Curio cabinets: These cabinets are ideal for displaying collectibles and personal items. Many come with adjustable shelves, lighting, and decorative molding.

Baskets, bins, and other ideas

Baskets: Various sizes of baskets are available for storing all kinds of items. These are often very decorative.

Bins: Storage solutions come in many shapes, colors, and sizes. I recommend that you look for bins and containers that can slide under beds and tables. That way, not only are you storing items, but you are also keeping them handy and out of sight.

Modular containers: These can be stacked to take advantage of vertical spaces.

How to Have a Successful Yard Sale

After you have de-cluttered and come up with storage solutions, you will need to get rid of everything you have decided to part with. A good way to use this to your advantage is to have a yard sale.

Applying the four Ps of marketing: Product, price, place, and promotion

In order to have a successful yard sale, you will need to know your product, set appropriate prices, find a place that will showcase your items, and promote your sale properly.

Product

Be organized

When selling books and compact discs, arrange them in a box with titles or artists facing upwards so the customers can easily read them. When these are in a big jumbled mess instead, it gives the impression that the sellers did not care about their belongings and probably didn't take good care of them when they owned them.

You can also sort small toys and put them in sealed clear plastic bags, according to the type of toy or age group. Then staple or tape the bags closed so customers cannot open them. Have a set price for the entire bag. Following your sale, these packages are then easy to transport for donations.

You will do fine even if you don't have a great deal of time to organize your stuff; there have been many successful yard sales with only one week's notice.

Make items appealing

Put some effort into your sale and really try to sell items by making them as attractive as they can be. If the first thing that someone picks up is dirty or otherwise unappealing, it may turn him or her off of looking at other things you have to sell. Make sure, for example, that your old basketball is full of air and that all clothes are washed and pressed.

Power it up

If an item needs batteries, put some in it so it actually works — this will help the object to sell. Instead of putting in brand new batteries, find some half-used ones, perhaps those from your remote controls. If you are selling a television set or other electronic equipment, have it turned on or at least plugged in, in case someone wants to check it out.

Keep image in mind

If all that people can see from the roadside is a tarp with a mountain of clothes heaped on top of it, they will likely drive on by. This vision is certainly not appealing. Ask friends or neighbors to loan you portable tables or card tables, if necessary.

Try to sort all of your items by categories; for example, kitchen goods on one table and games and toys on another. Just imagine going to a yard sale and seeing boxes of dirty, disorganized, and cobwebbed junk on the ground and the seller sitting there having his or her coffee, chatting with neighbors, and ignoring potential buyers. These people probably wonder why they never have successful yard sales. In keeping with staging your home, you need to stage your yard sale too!

Set the mood

Yard sales are more relaxing if there is some background music on. Have easy listening, middle-of-the-road type of music on, rather than heavy metal. This atmosphere allows a more relaxed shopping experience, puts your customers at ease, welcomes them to stay longer (thus spend more), and facilitates communication between you and your customers.

Attraction

People often drive around their neighborhoods on Saturday morning and seek out yard sales for their bargains. In order to pique their curiosity and lure them in, display some of your larger, more interesting or top-selling items at the end of your driveway. Some people will just drive by slowly and take a quick look to determine if your sale looks like it's worth stopping for, so entice them.

Where you should be

It may be a good idea for you, the seller, to be positioned closest to the street. This spot prevents people from "forgetting" to pay for an item on their way out and you are close enough to answer questions from people who drive by and ask, for example, "Do you have any LPs?"

All sales final

To avoid any issues later on, post a sign that reads "All Sales Final." There have been stories about customers returning the next day wanting their money back on curtains that didn't fit or end tables that were too big.

Appeal to everyone

Set items out in plain view of the road to attract those who wouldn't usually be interested in a yard sale. For example, while one person may love perusing the usual knick-knacks at a yard sale, another may be more attracted to a lawn mower or power tools. It is a good idea to set up tables targeted at those with particular interests. For example, set up a table with nothing but jars full of screws or nails, electronic parts, or tools. This strategy can give those who usually don't enjoy yard sales something to immerse themselves in while waiting for a treasure hunting partner, and it gives you additional sales.

Hide it or sell it

Make sure any items you do not want to sell are put away. If not, they will be the ones a buyer wants. Sometimes you just cannot win! Once a customer was adamant about buying a table that was used for display, but it was not for sale; it even had a tablecloth over it. Someone else wanted to buy the tablecloth! Now I just use plain sheets as table coverings. Of course, at a subsequent yard sale, I wanted to sell the table but couldn't!

Under cover

In order to hide items in my garage that weren't for sale, I stretched an inexpensive nylon rope around the walls, anchored it so it wouldn't droop, then put up sheets to hide my stuff. I used clothespins to hold the sheets to the rope. Of course, if you do not have clothespins, you can improvise and use binder clips.

Top it up

Throughout your sale, keep your sale tables attractive by filling up empty spots as items get sold.

Be careful how you arrange things

Be a little strategic in arranging your items. Use common sense and do not prop a nicely framed picture against a rocking chair on a very windy day — something that happened at a yard sale, and the seller had a lot of glass shards to clean up afterwards! Keep makeup, compact discs, and electronic equipment out of the sun, and keep clothing off the grass.

Ensure that all of your tables are stable and on even ground.

The following incident is a little bizarre, but it happened: It was a hot and sunny day and a seller had a makeup mirror on display. The brilliant reflection of the mirror caused a nearby cardboard box to catch on fire! Just keep this in mind.

Watch for potential profit loss

When selling clothing and coats, take a minute and go through the pockets. A buyer once found a $20 bill in a jacket that she paid $5 for.

Price

Display pricing

Ideally, put prices on everything. The price should be on top of an item, not on the bottom so customers won't have to manhandle (and risk breaking) anything. Pricing is a lot of work, but worth it because you won't have people asking you every two minutes, "How much do you want for this? " Additionally, if you are cohosting a yard sale, you won't undermine your friend's desired price, or vice versa.

Know how to price

As a general rule of thumb, price items about a quarter or a third of what they would cost new. However, there are exceptions. Clothes are generally very poor sellers, unless they are baby or kids' clothes. If you price adult-sized clothing cheap enough, it will sell regardless; people are reluctant to pay a lot of money for clothes they cannot try on, but are willing to take a gamble if it is only for a dollar or so. I recommend taking some of your "nicer" clothes to consignment stores, rather than trying to sell them at a yard sale. Remember, you can always mark down a price, but it's much harder to mark it back up.

Use organized pricing

If you do not have time to price everything individually, signs are helpful, such as "All books 25 cents each," "Each piece of clothing $1.00," or "Anything on this table 50 cents." You also can offer the customers a deal, for example, "Paperbacks 25 cents each or five for $1." Another suggestion is to categorize priced items by location in the yard; post a large, clear sign marked "All items $5.00" where the section is, and make sure it is quite obvious so that buyers aren't upset that they thought a $15 item was only $5.

Offer "fill a bag" deals

If you have a lot of kids' clothes or small toys that you want to get rid of, consider having a "fill a bag for a set price" kind of deal. Yard sale buyers love getting a good deal. I have seen yard sales with "fill a bag full of clothes for $2" and "fill a lunch bag with small toys for a nickel" (very cheap). They sold with great success. If you use this approach, ensure that you have enough bags available to do so.

Be objective when pricing

When pricing items, keep in mind that "a quarter or a third of what it costs new" is only a guideline. Unfortunately, buyers don't care that you paid $75 for your advanced quantum physics book ten years ago. Try to look at your items objectively: Do you really think people will be knocking down your door to get at your old t-shirts with stains on them? (They make excellent rags!)

If you still have the original boxes and instruction manuals for an item, you can probably charge a little bit more for it. Also, remember that one person's trash is another person's treasure; even if you think Aunt Edna's crocheted orange toilet seat cover deserves to go in the trash, it may be the first thing that sells!

If you have many items that have missing pieces or are broken, put them in a "FREE" box with a note "Broken — good for parts," or something to that effect.

Use pricing displays

Another suggestion about pricing is to consider the physical size of the item; the bigger the item, the larger the price tag should be. If you are selling a sofa, you cannot expect the buyer to be looking all over it for some tiny dot sticker, so make it obvious. Use a full sheet of paper, indicate the price, and list any good selling points or existing flaws. For example, "Sofa — $200 Firm — only three years old — comes with coordinating pillows." Another example could be a 3-inch by 5-inch card placed on a junky lawn mower at a yard sale, that says: "Lawn mower $5 — As is. Has fuel leak but starts." I've seen this, and it sold.

Watch the response to pricing

When I ask a seller how much he or she wants for a particular item, many times the person responds, "I don't know, how about 50 or 25 cents?" No buyer in his or her right mind would respond, "Yeah, I want to pay the higher price. Give it to me for 50 cents." The better way for a seller to respond would be, "How about 50 cents?" Then, if I were to put the item back or hesitate, the seller could counter offer with, "Or how about a quarter?" By approaching your customers with the higher price first, you give yourself room to negotiate.

Place

On your property

If you are planning to host the sale in your yard, rather than your driveway or garage, make sure the grass has been cut recently, but not too recently. You do not want big wet clumps of grass sticking to people's shoes. For safety reasons for all involved, fill in any ruts in the ground to prevent people from tripping. Also, if you are having a yard sale as opposed to a garage sale, and have a dog that routinely poops in your yard where you expect people to be walking around, keep an eye out and do some pooper-scooping before the sale.

Love me, love my dog

Although you may have the friendliest dog in the world, it is best to keep animals away from your yard sale. Some people are afraid of dogs or are allergic. The day of your yard sale may be the day that your friendly dog, unaccustomed to the excitement of all the people, decides to nip the toddler that pulls on his tail. Dogs may also jump up on customers and get mud on their pants. Keeping the dog out of sight is also for his or her own safety, since cars will be coming and going from your driveway.

Parking

Before deciding to have a yard sale at your house, consider whether you have adequate parking to handle an additional four or five cars parked near your house at one time. If not, consider suggesting to a good friend (who has plenty of parking at his or her house and has a prime yard sale location) if he or she would like to have a yard sale with you at his or her house. The trouble with this suggestion is that you could end up using all your yard sale profits to buy your friend's stuff, and vice versa!

Other options

You can also rent a table or space at a fund-raising yard sale put on by a local church, school, or civic group, not to mention community flea markets.

Promotion

Set a date

Most people have weekends off, so Saturdays and Sundays are usually the days devoted to being around the house or going out for leisurely drives. In other words, yard sales are ideally held on weekends. But do not pick a busy holiday weekend such as Thanksgiving or Labor Day to have your sale, as you'll generally have a better turnout if it is a non-holiday weekend. There are two possible exceptions to this rule. One, is if you live in a high tourist area (e.g., near a beach where you'd receive a lot of foot traffic), or two, on holiday weekends which usually involve a lot of car travelling (e.g. Mother's or Father's Day, when those driving by might have their curiosity piqued).

Keep in mind that most people are paid either weekly, biweekly, or on the first of each month. As such, it is hard to ensure a date that would accommodate everyone financially to ensure that they have disposable cash to spend at your sale. However, the end of the month seems to be a harder period than others. Remember, those on pensions or social assistance usually receive their checks at the beginning of each month. If you live in a rural area, where there are one or two major employers, you may consider timing your yard sale with their pay periods.

Free advertising

Go big and advertise your yard sale on the Internet, for free. There are several online sites that offer free advertising, such as www.kijiji.com, or www.craigslist.org, which is a comprehensive website listing everything you can imagine from everywhere; from California to Nova Scotia, and many other international destinations. Your community may even have its own website with free online classifieds.

Also put up advertisements on bulletin boards within your community, such as at grocery stores, community centers, libraries, and mailbox centres; spread the news of your yard sale via word of mouth to coworkers and friends; and post a sign in front of your home a few days before the big event.

Inexpensive paid ads

Advertise in your local newspaper. If you are unsure of what to say in your ad, read some others and copy bits and pieces from them; make sure to have proper spelling and your correct address. Ask your neighbors if they want to share the cost of the newspaper ad and hold a multifamily yard sale — the more, the merrier!

Sign restrictions or bylaws

Find out if your local government has any restrictions in place regarding yard sales or garage sales. Some municipalities may require a permit or may have a limit on how many yard sales a person is allowed to hold per year.

Be aware that there may also be laws regarding the placement of signage. Some areas are lax in the enforcement of these laws and others are strict. Some towns have laws that read something to the effect of: "It is illegal to post, without a city or county permit, private signs on a public right of way." "Public right of way" is commonly defined as both sidewalks on either side of a street and everything in between, including grassy medians, gutters, cement medians, traffic signs, lamp posts, trees, foliage, and fences.

If you live in a condominium, or elsewhere where there's a home owners' association, you may want to check if there are any restrictions regarding signage or yard sales.

Sign design

Make very clear yard sale signs. You'll find a couple of recommended designs in Appendix I.

One good idea is to go to a dollar store or your local office supply store and purchase black foamcore (it is approximately $\frac{1}{4}$-inch thick so it is sturdy enough). Cut the foamcore into signs in the shape of arrows. Then cut white paper the same shape as your sign, but a half inch smaller than the foamcore. Write your message on the paper in large, solid print and in capital letters. Keep in mind that you will only have four seconds to send your message to a driver passing by. Glue this onto the foamcore arrow. Keep in mind the direction you will be placing the sign on a post, ensuring that the direction of the arrow is indeed pointing towards your house.

Another way to make an effective sign is to draw it on a paper grocery bag, fill with rocks and newspaper, then staple shut. This makes an easy, portable sign that you can just place on the ground. If you use crayon to illustrate your signs, the lettering won't run if it gets wet. I use a permanent marker and make the lettering extra wide. Signs written in ballpoint pen are not effective!

It is helpful if all of your signs look similar. For example, using the same style of sign, the same colored lettering, or the same colored cardboard will prompt people to continue to follow your signs!

Writing your sign

When writing your sign, keep in mind the design of highway speed signs; they are black and white, clear, and simple, because you only have seconds to get the attention of people driving by. Similarly, your font (style of lettering), sign size, and the details in your sign need to be equally clear to get your message out to a driver.

Don't try to cram too many words on the signs. All that's really needed is the words "Yard Sale" (or "Garage Sale,") the date of the sale, the street address, and a bold arrow pointing the way.

It is important to allow your children to participate in your yard sale, but do not give them sign-making duties or you may have to redo the signs. Unless they can follow design suggestions and have the appropriate skill set, you risk having words that are too small to read from a car or that are in colors in which the message is not easily processed. Big bubble lettering adorned with flowers and butterflies may be attractive, but it is often illegible.

After your signs are up, drive past them to see if you can read them easily. If you can't, nobody else can either.

Posting signage

Put up signs in your neighborhood the evening before the sale (or a day or two before sale day) that directs customers to your house.

Avoid putting your signs on utility poles. The staples and nails used to affix the signs can pose a safety hazard to workers who have to climb the poles; nails and staples can tear safety equipment such as gloves, harnesses, and clothing (and hands, arms, and legs too). Depending on where you live, you could even be breaking the law by attaching signs to utility poles. If your area allows it, tape your posters to street signs or buy some inexpensive stakes and put your signs on those. Some communities have rules about posting yard sale signs on street signs, so make sure you follow these rules.

You can also use inexpensive wire landscaping fencing to make a sign (I often see it for sale at yard sales); cut sections of it apart, draw your sign on a paper bag, put the paper bag over the wire frame, and staple the bag closed at the bottom. I also think that nailing signs to trees is a big no-no!

Yard sale bargaining

Some buyers will expect you to barter with them. If it is early in the morning and you do not want to bargain, just say to them, "I think it is worth that price. I may lower the price later in the day if it doesn't sell."

Selling popular items

If you are trying to sell something that is fairly expensive and a popular item that appears in catalogs or sale ads, cut out the ad with the item in it (with the price showing, of course) and tape it to your item. I've seen this done mostly with gently used children's toys. It shows the buyer that spending $10 for an item that normally sells for $40 (new) is a great deal. Be selective if you use this tactic, as people will get turned off if you do it for every item you are trying to sell.

Early birds

Often, experienced yard sale buyers will arrive at your doorstep early in the morning to get the best deals; some sellers love them, others hate them. If you really do not want them, consider putting a disclaimer in your ad saying "NO EARLY BIRDS." Then, if people show up before your start time, just say, "Prices before (your scheduled start time) are doubled (or tripled)."

Some aggressive yard sale early birds have been known to "drop in" to your house the day before the sale, tell you they aren't able to come by the next day, and then ask to shop early. For the most part, these "birds" are experienced dealers who want to find diamonds in the rough that they can turn around and sell for a tidy profit in their antique stores.

If you've had problems in the past with early birds, you may want to just put the street name and block number in your newspaper ad; for example, "Yard sale in the 200 block of Elm Street." You may not mind some early birds who are only a little bit early, say 15 minutes or so, but you do not want people camped out at five o'clock in the morning in front of your house.

Money handling and sales

Change

Have lots of coins and small bills available to make change. If you do not, your first customer will be someone trying to buy 50 cents' worth of stuff with a $20 bill.

The amount of money you should start off with depends on the average prices of what you are selling. If you are selling a lot of small, lower priced items, you should be fine with around $80 to $100 broken down into small denominations. If you have a lot of furniture or higher priced items, definitely start with more money. For instance, if you have a lot of $10 items, most people will probably give you $20 bills and expect change. Of course, as the yard sale continues some people will give you the exact amount, so it is mostly in the beginning that you will need to be concerned about how much change to have on hand.

Giving change

If someone hands you a large bill, leave the bill out in view until after you have given him or her change. You can put the bill partly under something such as a paperweight until after you hand the person his or her change. Otherwise, a dishonest person could tell you that he or she gave you a $20 bill, not a $10 bill. It would be your word against that person's word. Also remember, you are going to be very busy and at times rushed when making change, so make sure you really take a moment and look at the bill — it is easy to make mistakes.

Having a calculator handy is helpful in totaling purchases. Make it easy for yourself to total items by pricing things evenly, for example 25 cents, 50 cents, and $1, instead of 40 cents, 75 cents, and $1.20.

Guard your money

Do not leave your money lying around in a box. I recommend wearing a fanny pack or carpenter's apron so you'll always have your money with you. However, when making change, keep the wad of bills in your fanny pack rather than pulling out a big wad of bills.

You may want to keep some bills separate if your fanny pack has several zippered compartments, or move some bills to another secret location in your home. If you are running out of change and someone is trying to haggle a cheaper price, be willing to negotiate if the buyer has the exact change.

Checks

Do not accept checks unless you are willing to take the risk of getting a bad check, which could cost you as much as $20 in some places, as well as the item you "sold." A check that looks perfectly fine may be from a closed bank account.

Total the items yourself

You may get a customer who wants to "help" you by totaling his or her purchases ahead of time and giving you the total. This may be a ploy to sneak another expensive item into his or her pile or to not pay the full amount of his or her purchase. If you encounter this tactic, just say that you need to go through each of their items because some of the things may be your cohost's and you want to divide the money fairly with the cohost.

High expectations

It is impossible to have the perfect yard sale. Some things are unpredictable, so you have to adjust quickly and go with the flow. For example, it is highly possible to run out of small bills even though you may have started with a lot of small bills and change at the beginning of your yard sale. It may seem that everyone wants to pay with a $20 bill. Or you could have underestimated the amount of grocery bags required to bag sold items.

Dealing with customers

Be honest

One of my pet peeves is when I'm looking at an item and a seller says, "Oh, that's new," when it is obviously something that was purchased in 1978, has a big stain on it, or is half-empty. Be honest with your customers.

Be discreet

It is a good idea to keep your eyes on your customers, but do not stare at them or hover inches away from them. It can get annoying when sellers are a little "too" overbearing and recount a story about each of their items to remind you what a good deal it is. This is easier said than done! It is easy to start rambling on to customers about why you are selling something even though they didn't ask you about it in the first place!

Watch what you say

Do not insult your customers. If customers are searching through clothes that you do not think are suitable for them, try to remember that they could be thinking of buying the items for other people. Refrain from suggesting alternatives for them.

Adding value

Keep customers hydrated

If your yard sale is blessed with a hot and sunny day, consider selling sodas or having the kids run a lemonade stand. It is generally easier to keep sodas cold, as you can put them on ice in a big cooler (bought on sale, of course). Just sell the kind of soda you like so you won't mind if you have leftovers. Selling lemonade can also be tricky for a five year old who doesn't understand a lot about hygiene and will want to just grab ice cubes with their hands. Someone told me she once saw a child stirring a pitcher of lemonade with his *arm*!

Offering complimentary paper cups filled with ice water on a hot day, with a trash can close by, is also a nice touch. The longer people stay at your yard sale, the more likely they will buy something. Even if they just stay and browse, it may lure others to the sale; nothing attracts a crowd like a crowd.

Bag it

Have plastic grocery bags available to bag sold items. If selling breakables, have newspaper available to wrap fragile items.

Hangers

Use everyday metal hangers if you are displaying clothes on a rack so that buyers can keep the hangers if they want to.

Get help

Collecting sale items

If you can, enlist friends or relatives to help you accumulate items you want to sell weeks before your yard sale. Put all the items in a designated area in some out-of-the-way place to sort and price.

Find a partner or cohost

If possible, invite a neighbor or friend to co-host or assist you at your yard sale. More hands make less work, and if you have a co-host, you can split the cost of a newspaper ad. The more stuff you have available to sell the better and more buyers mulling over items in your yard entices other people to stop by too.

Let your kids help

Involve your kids by getting them to set up their own table selling old toys. As encouragement, you can remind them that if they get rid of their old outgrown toys, they will make space for newer items they can buy with the money they earn. You may have to help them with pricing; they may want to overprice an item that could sell well if it was priced cheaper. The goal of a yard sale is to lighten your load by selling everything and not taking any of it back into your home. Your child will learn lessons about earning money, managing money, and the art of de-cluttering. Plus you'll have help and more space! It's a win-win situation.

Safety tips

Protect yourself and others with these safety tips:

- If you are trying to sell old kitchen utensils, cover the knives with rubber bands so people do not cut themselves.

- Have a cellular or cordless phone with you at all times.

- If you are selling electrical appliances, place them close to an electrical outlet (if possible) or have a long extension cord handy. Put the cord away when you're not using it to show a customer an item — you do not want to create a tripping hazard.

- Do not allow strangers into your house to try out appliances or try on clothes. If someone needs to use a rest room, give the person directions to the nearest gas station or fast-food restaurant.

- Before your sale, look through the boxes of everything you want to sell. On occasion, items have been sold with old credit card receipts that were left in shoe boxes or used in books as bookmarks.

- Unfortunately, even at yard sales, it is important to protect yourself from those who prey on busy, preoccupied sellers. Ensure that your most valuable items are positioned wisely to minimize their risk of vanishing.

After the sale

Donations

Plan to donate good, unsold items to charities so that others will benefit. Confirm with charities first to see what kinds of donations they take, and in what condition the items should be.

eBay

If you still have some valuable items to sell, consider selling them on eBay, an online auction site. Visit http://pages.ebay.com/help/sell/index.html for a wealth of information to help you do this.

Be polite

Do not forget to take your signs down right after the sale. Neighbors resent unnecessary clutter in their neighborhood.

Success

Count your money; you will have just had a successful yard sale!

CHAPTER 6

REAL HOME STAGING EXAMPLES

To get the most out of this chapter, install the CD included with this book on your Windows-based PC and have a look at the example images.

Examples of Specific Areas

Curb appeal

Evaluation

The first impression of a property's exterior should be that of "welcome home." I once staged a home that was only four years old but did not appear that young. It was bad enough that winter made the landscape look dead, but the combination of the worn front deck and the dark paint color made the house look old and tired. See the before photo on the CD, under **Curb Appeal**.

Transformation

Spring provided the opportunity to lighten the house's color scheme. The dark hunter green color from the '90s not only dated the house but it also made a dark and unwelcoming impression. Changing shutters and decking, and painting the door a gray/blue color updated and freshened the overall look and feel. The gray/blue stairway drew the eye up to the front door, which should be the focal point. Painting the railings white created balance, brightened the front, and also helped make the door the focal point. Coordinated hardware such as a kick plate, light fixtures, numbers, door handles, and locks added richness and "bling."

Expanding the garden not only added more color, but also made it a better scale for the house and improved the view from the road. See the after photo on the CD, under **Curb Appeal**.

Front entrance

Evaluation

One home I staged had an entrance that was a large open space, and yet it was still cramped. The carpet restricted where a person could feel comfortable standing, while the large wildcat in the corner prevented the door from opening completely. The deacon's bench was full and was surrounded by shoes, creating a cluttered space. The swag above the door was decor from the early '90s, a dated look that would not suit many people's decorating taste. See the before photo on the CD, under **Entranceway**.

Transformation

All coats, shoes, and furnishings were removed and a vignette was created to welcome guests. The mirror was placed 90 degrees to the window to reflect the light into the space and the area rug was removed. A bouquet of flowers on a table to place keys and mail was a friendly welcome. See the after photo on the CD, under **Entranceway**.

Living Room

Evaluation

In another home, the original layout of the living room wasn't arranged to accommodate free traffic flow. Furnishings prevented easy access to the door that lead to the deck and drapes made it difficult to determine just where that door was. The furniture was arranged to accommodate the vast size of the room, but this resulted in a distant arrangement that wasn't a cozy or intimate environment. See the before photos on the CD, under **Living Rooms 1, 2, and 3.**

Transformation

The layout of a living room should enable buyers to see and have access to all its best features. You want them to be immediately drawn to the very features that make the property special.

One room was large enough to create two focal points: The first brought attention to the beautiful lake view and the second to the fireplace. After the entranceway, the living room makes an important impression and sets up expectations of the remainder of the house.

It is important that potential buyers instantly feel at home. To accomplish this in the space, the furniture was arranged into an intimate conversation area that accommodated

Be sure to have a welcoming entrance. After being drawn in by the curb appeal, buyers should be impressed once more with another "Hello!" once they are inside. The foyer should tell the buyers, "Welcome! We are expecting you, please make yourself at home!" A soft rug, a table with a lit lamp on it, some fresh flowers, and a bowl of wrapped candy lets the visitors know that they were thought of. Most importantly, a space should be left on the table for the real estate flyer/brochure, which can be placed on an easel or in a basket. In the homes we've staged, this special greeting has impressed many a realtor and seller!

Mark and Leslie Hoyt
Hello Home!, SC

traffic flow. See the after photos on the CD, under **Living Rooms 1, 2, and 3.**

Kitchen

Evaluation

A memorable kitchen I staged was desperately asking to be de-cluttered. A large, overgrown plant closed in the space, the counters were barely visible, and it was difficult to see the enormity of its storage space. The faux-finish paint job was outdated and really didn't emphasize the cabinets, but instead blended them into the wall. See the before photo on the CD, under **Kitchen**.

Transformation

This kitchen was painted Ivory Beige, and the backsplash was painted Soft Copper to coordinate with the floor and counter. The lighter color above the cabinets and clear counters opened the space. After this photo was taken, a bouquet of flowers was placed on the left side of the counter to add life and two stools were placed at the extended counter to show off a feature that would not otherwise be noticed. See the after photo on the CD, under **Kitchen**.

Master Bedroom

Evaluation

The master bedroom used in this example was chosen for its uniqueness. The room was 20 feet by 16 feet and L-shaped with five sets of windows and a spectacular view of the lake. The unique challenge in this room was the greeting by a half wall near the entrance that felt like a barrier upon entry. It was installed to create a headboard and prevented the use of a bed for a focal point at the facing wall. See the before photo on the CD, under **Master Bedroom.**

Transformation

Potential buyers typically buy into a lifestyle in the master bedroom, so give them serenity, peace, and quiet. Keep in mind that this is the place your potential buyer will be sleeping every night — so spoil them with its potential.

In this master bedroom, I broke the rules used in typical rooms because the bed was not used as a focal point. Instead I used the windows, which dominated the space with their breathtaking view upon entry to the room, as this was a huge selling feature. Anything that did not have a distinct purpose in the space was removed to eliminate any distraction. Drapes and window screens were removed and stored in the basement to open the space, maximize the light, and enhance the view.

In typical situations the whole room would have been painted a neutral color, but this room was very big and time was of the essence. Instead, the half wall positioned in

Most master bedrooms have exercise equipment in them. Every morning you wake up to realize that you are out of shape. Every evening you go to bed staring at a reminder that you did nothing that day to get in shape. How demoralizing. The bedroom should be staged as a retreat.

Michelle Finnamore
Advantage Staging, ON

the middle of the room was painted Ivory Beige to lighten its heavy visual presence. See the after photo on the CD, under **Master Bedroom.**

Master bathroom

Evaluation

This master bathroom was somewhat bland. There was nothing very exciting about it. The white paint chosen for the walls had a gray undertone and made the room feel cold. The use of blue curtains and towels next to the stark white made the space feel unbalanced. See the before photo on the CD, under **Master Bathroom.**

Transformation

Although blue is one of the most popular colors, it is always the first color to go when preparing a home for sale; it has so many variations that it is hard to pick the right shade for room conditions. It is very easy to make a room feel very cold with blue.

In keeping with the trend for bathrooms right now, I created a spa look and feel with white, chrome, glass, and mirror, to bring together a crisp, clean room, which is what you want for a bathroom. A few decorative touches were also placed to tie the room together and create a place where potential buyers could treat themselves. Fortunately for this home owner, privacy was not an issue, so the drapes were removed to allow more light to enter the room. If this is not possible in your situation, remove the curtain rod only for viewings and open houses. See the after photo on the CD, under **Master Bathroom.**

Dining room

Evaluation

I encountered a dining room that would have turned buyers off because it looked like there was not enough space. This was a big problem, as it is important that buyers are able to imagine their family and friends gathering in this room for dining, special occasions, and social time — and this would not have been possible in this room. It was overcrowded and cluttered. See the before photo on the CD, under **Dining Room.**

Transformation

A dining room should look and feel warm, inviting, and spacious. Once baby and personal items were removed, the walls were painted the staging-safe color Ivory Beige. Soft Copper was painted on one wall to coordinate with the flooring, which was a fixed item. The light fixture was updated to accommodate the style of the house, and the plants, buffet, and antique sewing machine were removed to allow for more space. The table was moved away from the breakfast bar and angled to allow freedom of movement and easy access to the outside deck. See the after photo on the CD, under **Dining Room.**

Bedrooms

Evaluation

In another home, one of the bedrooms was very small and needed to be kept simple to allow for freedom of movement. Generally, this would mean keeping minimal furniture and decorations in the room. See the before photo on the CD, under **Bedrooms.**

Transformation

The only solution for this small bedroom was to position a single bed under the window and use it as part of the focal point to accentuate the beautiful windows that were exposed after the drapes were removed. Only one medium-sized picture, framed to match the black furnishings, was hung to create a balance.

The bed became the focal point and the curtains were removed to show off the windows and allow more light to enter the room. See the after photo on the CD, under **Bedrooms.**

Main bathroom

Evaluation

In this bathroom, what seemed to stand out was someone's used bath towel and some personal decorations. See the before photo on the CD, under **Main Bathroom.**

Transformation

Main bathrooms are not that much different from the master bathroom. They should feel warm, serene, and luxurious.

In this bathroom, items of personal use were stored away and a towel bar was installed to accommodate luxurious towels. The wooden towel bar was chosen to coordinate with the pre-existing toilet-paper holder; otherwise, I would have suggested chrome or brushed nickel to follow current trends.

Upon entering the room, the presence of dated pink ceramic tiles was diminished with an oversized bath mat. It did not hide them, but prevented them from dominating the space.

A couple of pictures were hung to create balance in the space and a few towels were folded and placed on the back of the toilet to suggest a spa feeling. See the after photo on the CD, under **Main Bathroom.**

Hallways and stairways

Evaluation

It is important buyers concentrate on viewing the house and not where they are walking. It is best to simplify the space and keep main traffic areas free of obstructions. The hallway in a client's home was located at the end where it turns into the kitchen. It had become the location where items were collected to be taken out of the house, or placed there to be put away "later." Additionally, the bulletin board and its many papers created a chaotic feel in the small space.

Transformation

After stored items were returned to their rightful place, the desk was put on an angle to prevent it from impeding on the space. The bulletin board was removed and replaced with a light-colored picture to create warmth without visual weight, which would close in a small space. The door to the laundry room was closed to keep the space visually calm. See the before and after photos on the CD, under **Hall**.

Closets

Evaluation

One closet that I staged in a master bedroom seemed crowded and cramped. See the before photo on the CD, under **Closet 3.**

Transformation

The clothing in this closet was reduced to allow breathing space between the hangers. After all, in a perfect world this is how clothes would be hung. Clothing on shelves were folded and stacked neatly like you would find in a clothing store. The valance was removed from the window to brighten the area and allowed for a bright, fresh feeling closet. See the after photo on the CD, under **Closet 3**. The CD also has example photos of a spare/guest room closet and a closet in a bedroom where there was just enough clothing to display its available space. See the photos under **Closets 1 & 2**.

Examples of Staging Techniques

Create a lasting impression

The entrance can give one of the top three lasting impressions that will make or break any chance you have of receiving an offer.

Evaluation

In this example, the plant was dropping dead leaves onto the floor and there was nothing very exciting about the space. There was no strong motivator present to encourage anyone to explore the house. See the before photo on the CD, under **Impression.**

Transformation

In this space, I needed to make the viewer feel the immediate need to go into the living room to see the breathtaking view of the lake. The area was kept simple to allow the view to be a focal point. The vertical space was filled using twigs and glass beads in a glass cylinder vase, with a hint of the holiday given by a poinsettia. See the after photo on the CD, under **Impression.**

Create a focal point

Every room needs to have a focal point to attract interest. It is used in staging to enhance a room's best features.

Evaluation

In this example, the fireplace was not being used to highlight what a warm and inviting place a living room should be. This was one of the best features of the room, and yet it was lost and only used for practical reasons. See the before photo on the CD, under **Focal**.

Transformation

This living room was large enough to create two sitting areas. A focal point was formed on the opposite corner of the room using a large television armoire and a reading area was created to bring attention to the fireplace. The height of the brick and ceiling was highlighted with a tall, brass-framed mirror to coordinate with the fireplace. In keeping with scale, a topiary tree and tall candlesticks flanked the fireplace to offer warmth and balance. See the after photo on the CD, under **Focal.**

Expose special features

When preparing a home for sale, it is important to establish the features in each room that would be beneficial to highlight. The following examples are of a kitchen and a storage room.

Evaluation

When I staged the kitchen in this example, I recognized that it was impressive but lacked the "wow" factor. It appeared common with its everyday-living clutter, which created a very hectic, stressful impression and ruined the viewer's ability to see the vast counter space.

This kitchen was fitted with a wall oven, a built-in microwave, a countertop stove, a dishwasher, an additional island sink, and a special custom baker's countertop to be used for food preparation. However, none of this could immediately be seen when entering the room. See the before photos on the CD, under **Features 1 and 2**.

Transformation

The room was cleared of all paperwork and clutter. The space above the cabinets and countertops was cleared and only a couple of decor items were left in the room, to allow the eye to rest on areas that would help buyers see the size and scale of the room. Distractions were removed to allow an immediate view of all that this kitchen had to offer. A desk in the far corner, a custom baker's countertop, and a hidden bookcase under the countertop were all revealed. See the after photos on the CD, under **Features 1 and 2.**

Evaluation

Initially, you would not think that it was important to clear out a storage room. I once encountered a basement storage room that was set up to be a workshop. The room was not used for its intended purpose and was overcrowded.

Transformation

After the vast majority of the room's contents were packed and stored in another area of the house, it was revealed that this storage area of the basement was plumbed for a bathroom. This is a feature that could have been of interest to potential home buyers because there was no bathroom in the basement at that time.

Remove window screens and drapes

Removing window screens and drapes creates a dramatic impact when more light is needed in a space, and makes a considerable contribution to the overall impression of a room.

Evaluation

In one bedroom, the window treatments were sheer but diminished the light enough to make it darker than it needed to be. See the before photo on the CD, under **Drapes 1**.

Transformation

The large size of this master bedroom was already evident, but it was the view that needed the most attention when buyers entered the room. To emphasize the view, belongings were relocated to allow buyers to walk freely towards the awesome view, which could be easily seen through the large windows once the drapes and window screens were removed. See the after photo on the CD, under **Drapes 1.**

Evaluation

In another room, the drapes hid the beautiful natural oak windows and trim. See the before photo on the CD, under **Drapes 2**.

Transformation

The little girl who occupied this room loved the drapes, but they had to be removed to appeal to the vast majority of buyers. Without the drapes, the beauty of the windows was exposed; however, the blinds installed inside the frame of the window remained because privacy was an issue (although, they did not inhibit the view or diminish light in the room). See the after photo on the CD, under **Drapes 2**.

Neutralize personal taste

Bedrooms should be a place of calm and serenity. Although the occupant of a room may love his or her space, there are times personal style can prevent the majority of potential home buyers from entering a room.

Evaluation

One bedroom in particular had a gorgeous view of the lake but couldn't be seen past the extreme decor. The client's teenage daughter loved her bedroom so much she was distraught at the thought of having to paint over it. However, the three vibrant colors she sponge painted on the walls were overwhelming and would have discouraged interested buyers from entering the room to discover the hidden gem. In one home that I staged, the room's decor could have made a buyer miss the beautiful lake view. See the before photo on the CD, under **Neutral**.

Transformation

This house did not need to sell lifestyle; it was sold as soon as one entered the home. Therefore, the strategy behind this room was to keep it plain so that it would allow the window and its view to become the focal point.

Walls were painted Ivory Beige, which has a yellow undertone that coordinated well with the wood trim. All personal items were packed and removed from the room. Furniture was arranged to create an unobstructed view of the window, and curtains were removed to show off the view and allow more light to enter. A blanket was placed across the bed to direct the eye directly to the window.

The mirror was placed 90 degrees from the window to better reflect light into the room and draw more attention to the focal point. See the after photo on the CD, under **Neutral.**

Lighten up

Sometimes it is necessary to lighten a room so that the color is not so overwhelming.

Evaluation

A client's little girl created her "princess" bedroom using a shade of pink that was too strong on the walls, flower borders with various colors, and heavy drapes covering the windows. Her stuffed animals were also displayed among many other objects creating a very overwhelming space. The room felt small and closed in.

The little girl who slept in this bedroom was in love with it, as she had decorated it herself. See the before photo on the CD, under **Lighten**.

Transformation

Unfortunately, to make the room of interest to everyone viewing the home, most of its personality had to go. This room was the smallest in the house so it needed to be kept light in color. The room was painted a staging-safe neutral color, Ivory Beige, to go well with the yellow undertones of the wood trim.

Much of the room's contents were packed and stored in another area of the house and items that would be needed every day were arranged in the furnishings that remained in the room. The deep, dark dresser and mirror were placed 90 degrees from the window to bring more light into the bedroom.

Light-colored bedding was used to minimize the visual presence of the bed, which was placed in the middle of the room to give the feeling of a larger space. See the after photo on the CD, under **Lighten**.

Keep an eye on peripheral vision

Peripheral vision is the part of your vision that is outside the very center of what you are fixing your eyes on.

Evaluation

The deep, dark dresser in the bedroom in this example intruded on peripheral vision when viewing the room. This can create the sense of a barrier and distract the eye from a focal point. The matching desk and chair also acted as visual barriers. See the before photo on the CD, under **Vision**.

Transformation

I generally keep everything with visual weight lower than 4½-feet tall to keep from imposing on viewers' peripheral vision. However, the little girl occupying this room needed the remaining items. Therefore, the desk and bookcase were moved from the opposite wall and placed near the entrance. The second desk was relocated, which opened the space and eased traffic flow. See the after photo on the CD, under **Vision**.

Open traffic flow

Traffic flow is something that most people forget to consider when arranging their furnishings. The primary consideration for furniture arrangement is usually entertainment and conversation. However, selling a home means sacrificing some conveniences to accommodate free traffic flow. It is important that buyers can move throughout the space without the distraction of watching their step. Prepare your family; you may have to

sacrifice the television if it is located in the living room, particularly if it is a 50-inch television that eats up a large portion of the room.

Evaluation

In this room the doors to the deck, which looked out at the view, were obstructed with furnishings. There was also no clear path identified, which hindered traffic flow. See the before photo on the CD, under **Traffic**.

Transformation

The stunning view of the lake was used as the focal point in this living room. The space was large enough to create two intimate seating areas and still leave a path open between them to move freely towards the doors to the deck. The composition of the room directed the eye immediately to the windows, which could also be seen from the entrance to the house. See the after photo on the CD, under **Traffic**.

Use angles

Use angles as a strategy to direct the buyer to another location of the property, to highlight a feature of the home, or to accommodate a difficult layout. When using angles, it is important to remember to make them all the same or the room will feel awkward.

Evaluation

I once encountered a condo unit with several challenges that would require the use of angles. The rooms were built using six different angles and there was an open space in front of the windows that didn't have a sense of purpose. It would have been very difficult for a potential buyer to know what to do with this space. See the before photo on the CD, under **Angles**.

Transformation

In this space, I wanted potential buyers to be strongly attracted to the windows when they entered the room, as there was an awesome ocean view (which was a primary selling feature of the unit). To accomplish this, I chose one angle in the living room and arranged all the furnishings to accommodate that angle. A breakfast nook was set up to fill the space in front of the windows and suggest one potential use of the space, which would get viewers to imagine enjoying their morning meal in the sunshine or enjoying a relaxing, romantic dinner in front of the ocean view. There were just enough furnishings to provide a sense of purpose without compromising the feeling of spaciousness in the open concept area. To further enhance the room, three mirrors that emulated the windows were placed together above the sofa at 90 degrees to reflect light into the room. I also used the rule of three when placing candle bowls on the coffee table (which also coordinated with the glass bubbles in the lamps). See the after photo on the CD, under **Angles**.

Define the space

A common statistic often quoted in real estate is that only 10 percent of the population can see potential in a property, so do not make buyers rely on their imagination when looking at a room. You have to define the space so that they can immediately imagine how they could use it.

Evaluation

One room I staged was in the basement of a two-story house and was used as a home office, a TV room, and a play area. In other words, it was a dumping ground. Surprisingly, rooms like these are commonly found in many houses; however, I still wouldn't advise you to leave a room like this. Put in the effort to organize and arrange it properly. See the before photo on the CD, under **Space**.

Transformation

To define the space, begin by assessing your target market. There is already a living room upstairs. Would it be better to set this room up as an exercise room? A workshop? A family room?

It just so happened that in this example, there already was a full-service gym in the neighborhood. The room would have been perfect for a workshop, but since the neighborhood had a high school down the road, the house would likely be most attractive to a family with teens. This means they would probably be looking for more living space.

In the transformation, many items were packed and put into storage. The sofa was

---

Although I stage with the belief that you should not sterilize your occupied home from *all* of your personal pictures, I do believe that there needs to be *no more* than three in any particular room.

Often the walls, mantels, and shelves are so filled with personal photos that it distracts the buyers from the house. When it is so overwhelming, buyers feel as if they are being intrusive while viewing a home.

Connie Tebyani
Platinum Home Staging, Inc., CA

moved to the smaller living room upstairs and the darker furniture was moved into this room where it fit much better, as the space accommodated both its size and the heaviness of the dark color.

Although yellow is usually a color that people love (or at least tolerate), the shade will determine whether or not it should be replaced. In this room the shade was too stark and bold, and was changed to the staging-safe color Ivory Beige.

It is usually a good idea to remove personal photos; however, in this example they were presented as art and were appropriate for a family room.

The room was balanced using the tree in one corner and a plant on top of the armoire. The rocking chair was placed opposite the sofa to further balance the room. See the after photo on the CD, under **Space**.

Suggest a use

Evaluation

Aside from the master bedroom, a basement is often the most neglected part of a house. In most cases, the added space is not given any sense of purpose. Suggesting a use can provide ideas for potential home buyers who may not know what to do with a space, such as the one in this example. See the before photo on the CD, under **Use**.

Transformation

The area was large enough to create two "rooms" to suggest an in-law suite and an added family room for playing board games and a children's play area.

Plants were relocated and toys were organized and placed in the opposite corner (which cannot be seen in the photo). A rug that was removed from the living room was relocated to this space to create a cozy, defined area. Two pink reclining chairs that were also removed from the living room were set up with an old dining table to imply that the space could be used to play board games. See the after photo on the CD, under **Use**.

Sell a lifestyle

Evaluation

A vacant two-bedroom, 2,000 square-foot condominium was on the market for $497,000; the upper portion of market values in the area. This was an occasion to stage the unit using a lifestyle strategy. The power of suggestion of use of space and imagining what it would be like to live in the unit would influence the decision to put in an offer. Otherwise, it would generally be difficult for anyone to imagine what to do with this particular vacant space. See the before photo on the CD, under **LIFESTYLE**.

Transformation

In this room, the table was staged to create an ambiance that could be set for either breakfast or dinner; it would sell the space as a great place to wake up in the morning or relax after work. Now viewers could imagine coming home from a stressful day at work and treating themselves to dinner overlooking the cityscape, which is of particular beauty after dark. Or they could imagine waking up on the weekend to enjoy a relaxing breakfast and morning newspaper, especially in the winter months when this area of the condo receives plenty of sunlight, warmth, and brightness. See the after photo on the CD, under **LIFESTYLE**.

Dress up for the occasion

When you prepare a room for pictures, open houses, or showings, always dress the bed with ironed, fine linen, that is displayed neatly. Fold down the top sheet and layer the bed with pillows to provide a look of luxury. A well-dressed bedroom in a $150,000 or $500,000 home, will create a positive response because it represents a desired lifestyle.

Evaluation

It is difficult to buy into a lifestyle setting such as a bedroom in a luxury condo when it is vacant. There is nowhere for the eye to rest and lacks the appeal of a desired lifestyle. See the photo on the CD under **Dress**.

Transformation

This bed was outfitted with ironed, fine linen and was layered with pillows. A bed skirt was a necessity to complete the look. I folded a black single sheet and tucked it under the gold top sheet to border it and to coordinate with the black pillows (which were used to harmonize with the black used in the furniture). Ironing the sheets, pillow cases, and covers can give a look of refinement even if you do not have fine linen. Make the added effort and you will see a dramatic difference.

The bed used in this vacant staging was an inexpensive mattress and had hard corners. I used a plush duvet under the fitted sheet to emulate a luxurious bed. A plush comforter would create a similar look, but for this room I wanted to use this quilt for its fine material and color. A tray displayed with what could be breakfast provided a finishing touch to this guest bedroom. See the after photos on the CD, under **Dress**.

Show scale in vacancies

One would believe that an empty room would feel larger, but vacancy actually works against the seller because there is nothing there to show scale. Rooms will look and feel much smaller than they really are.

Evaluation

In this example, the room was small and it was hard to tell if a queen bed could fit. It was hard to tell if it would accommodate two occupants or a child. See the before photo on the CD, under **Vacant**.

Transformation

Value is added to a two-bedroom property when a small bedroom is displayed to show double occupancy. This bedroom was arranged with just a double bed, two night tables, and two lamps, enough furniture to display scale and lifestyle. See the after photo on the CD, under **Vacant**.

Be creative

It does not matter what you do to prepare, there will always be something that will create a challenge for you. There will be times when you will need to break the rules and just do what the situation calls for. Improvise with what you have to work with.

Evaluation

Before the bedroom in this example was transformed, it was the type of bedroom seen in most typical homes whereby it was always the last to get attention. It lacked a headboard and focal point. The walls were quite damaged from years of moving wall hangings and everyday living. A large picture is usually placed above the headboard of a bed to create a focal point, but in this case, the home owner did not want any nail holes placed in the freshly painted walls.

Transformation

Given that holes were not to be put into the walls, the only picture I hung was a large wall hanging above the bed, which was used to create a strong focal point. Without a headboard to establish a focal point and as an alternative to putting holes into the wall, a headboard was created using two standard-size pillows standing tightly against the wall. The fitted sheet from the bedding set was draped over the pillows to coordinate with the folded down top sheet. See the photo on the CD, under **Creative**.

Create more space

If you have lived in a house for a long time and have accumulated many favorite things along the way, it can be difficult to pack them up — particularly if you are continuing to live in the home while it is on the market. It will feel strange to continue living in the house you called home when it no longer feels like home, but I promise you, it is worth it.

Evaluation

The dining room in this example was used as a home office and as a place for piano practice, and collections made up most of the decor. The curtains obstructed the quality of the windows and casings, which would be of interest to potential buyers. See the before photo on the CD, under **More Space**.

Transformation

The collections and extra furnishings were removed to make more space to move throughout the room. The dining room table was angled to direct traffic flow from the far entryway to the kitchen. The window dressings were also removed to expose the windows and their frames, and the desk, computer, and other random contents were relocated. See the after photo on the CD, under **More Space**.

Keep it simple

Evaluation

Keeping an area simple will highlight a property's best features and allow potential buyers to imagine their own belongings in the space.

The clutter in this kitchen diminished any chance of impressing a buyer. See the before photo on the CD, under **Simple**.

Transformation

The entire area was cleared of clutter and items were packed away in boxes or in cabinets to create a sense of calm and to expose the features of the kitchen. The table was positioned to maximize freedom of movement in the breakfast nook and to offer full access to the lake view. All that remained in the room was a hint of the holiday season, a vase of red and white poinsettias, and a bowl of fruit. See the after photo on the CD, under **Simple**.

CHAPTER 7

HOW TO LOOK FOR GOOD PROFESSIONALS

When to Hire a Professional Home Stager

I believe that anyone can stage a home adequately with a few proven techniques, and a lot of hard work. However, there are several occasions when you may need to call in a professional:

- You are uncertain about your ability to accomplish the extraordinary presentation that your situation demands.

- You may need to sell quickly, be selling in an extremely competitive market, or be selling a very high-end home and need to exceed the expectations of a high-end lifestyle.

- You are selling a vacant property. Empty properties take much longer to sell because there is nothing there for viewers to get emotionally involved with, there is no impression of scale, and there is no suggestion of how to arrange furnishings in the space. You can still stage it yourself by borrowing or renting furniture, or using your own furnishings, but it will be a lot of work. Stagers usually have their own inventory and accessories or have access to furniture rentals. Rental may even be cheaper through a professional.

- You are too busy. If time is of the essence and you are not able to dedicate time and energy to prepare for selling, consider hiring a professional.

- You do not have help. If you are among the many people who do not have a support network that is prepared to help you, because your children have moved away, or because you are living away from family and close friends, consider hiring a professional to assist you.

- You have physical limitations. Staging is a very laborious undertaking and can involve moving furniture from one room or level to another. If you have a bad back, are not physically up to the job, or have other physical limitations, consider hiring a professional.

- You have allergies. Packing up a home, especially when you have not moved in a while, can accumulate dust in places you never thought possible. The process of staging can stir up a lot of dust causing some major problems with individuals who suffer from allergies. If this is the case, be sure to run an air purifier while doing the work (or request that your stager do so if you have hired one to do the work instead).

How to Hire a Professional Home Stager

What makes a home stager a professional?

Ask a home stager what makes him or her qualified for your particular job. Certifications are an indication of expertise, but there are stagers with many years of experience that will have a fabulous portfolio to verify their level of excellence. Ask if the stager belongs to RESA or any other trade associations and decide if you are comfortable with his or her answer.

Remember, you are choosing someone to go into your home and to possibly go through your private belongings (should you request a full staging job). See if you feel comfortable with the stager and whether or not he or she is confident with their business. Here is a list of indicators to consider:

- If you are meeting with the stager in person, is the person dressed appropriately for a presentation?

- If the stager is visiting with you directly after staging another house, does he or she look presentable?

If you are going to hire a professional home stager to give you an opinion on how to get the most equity out of your property, please listen to him or her with an open mind. The job of a home stager is to increase the profit on your property. The stager's success is gauged by how quickly the property sells and the money made on the sale. He or she is on the client's side and will make suggestions that will benefit the seller.

As the old saying goes:

"Doctor, Doctor, it keeps hurting when I do this."

"Well, stop doing it."

Michelle Finnamore
Advantage Staging, ON

- If the stager is meeting you in your home, how does the person make you feel?

- If the person references your house, is he or she speaking with respect?

- If you are talking over the phone, is the stager giving you his or her full attention?

Look at their service structure

Professional stagers are pretty flexible and will offer the opportunity to choose what best suits your needs. You should be able to select from a variety of options, it does not have to be all or nothing.

Find out if they offer a contract

Most contracts for stagers are not complicated and more or less describe a list of expectations from both parties. A good contract will be typed, legible, and easy to read, and will protect you and your stager. There should be no fine print.

Look at their portfolio

Good home stagers are proud of their work and should have their portfolio available for you to view immediately on request, whether in person or on their website.

Ask if the photos are of their own work

It is likely that most stagers only present their own work in the portfolio they are showing you; just to be sure, you can ask them about it and see if you can call the owners of the houses in the photos.

Call references

Do not rely on the fact that the stager offered you a couple of references. Actually call the people who hired this person previously. They will not mind that you called. In fact, they will want to brag about their new experience, if it was a good one.

Actually talking to a person who has used the services of a professional home stager you are looking into hiring is the best way to find out whether or not you should hire the stager. Here are examples of questions you should ask:

- Was the person respectful of your feelings and your belongings?

- Was the home stager punctual?

- Did the person work alone or bring in someone to help?

- Did the home stager provide a contract?

- Were the service fees what the person quoted?

- Did you have the option to stay during the staging or were you asked to leave?

Ask to see testimonials

If you are relying on the Yellow Pages, newspaper advertisements, or the Internet, ask to see the stager's list of testimonials. These should also be available on the stages's website (if he or she has one); consider it a "red flag" if there are no testimonials.

Compare quotes

Time spent staging a house varies with every property and every stager has his or her own way of coming up with a quote. As with most trades, the most economical quote is not necessarily the best one. Compare what services are included, the time allotted for the job, and when the stager can start. Also find out how accurate the quote is, and if it is a reliable estimate of what you should expect to pay at the end of the job.

Keep in mind that there is no black and white answer to how much a home stager will cost. First, you need to remember that staging is not a cost, but an investment; you will make your money back and more. Second, it is very difficult to determine exactly how much you can expect to pay.

Look into their code of ethics

Many professional stagers belong to a trade association that has a code of ethics that they are required to adhere to. Ask for the website where you can view it or ask for a copy to read.

Ask for recent success stories

Home staging is a proven, effective tool for selling and good home stagers will have a few success stories that they are excited about that they will tell you right away. Consider it a red flag if they hesitate and unenthusiastically tell you a story.

How much does a professional home stager cost?

There are many factors that will affect how much you will pay to use a professional home stager's services:

- **Location:** An urban property will likely cost more than a rural one, solely based on volume and demand. This is just a fact of life. Factors that affect the housing market will also affect home stagers' pricing, such as the location within your country, state or province, or city. There are some staging organizations that are trying to regulate pricing so that everyone pays a similar price, but as I said previously, it is a young industry and it is still in development.

- **Experience:** It is likely that a more experienced stager will charge more than one who is just starting out and wants to develop his or her portfolio. Determine whether your property is in need of an extraordinary display or if the services of a beginner will be sufficient.

- **Talent:** It is easy to assume that experience would naturally bring talent, but that is not the case. Creative thinking and talent cannot be taught. Good stagers will charge more for their services, just as anyone in other trades would.

- **Labor:** The amount of time and labor needed will affect the outcome of a quote. If the job is a large one, you may need to hire more stagers or helpers.

- **Inventory:** We insiders refer to accessories and furnishings as props or inventory. There are stagers who include these in their fees, but most prefer to charge a rental fee for those used (per room or individually).

Depending on your location, you can expect to pay as little as $100 for a consultation in which the home stager will give you a detailed analysis of your property and advise you how best to prepare your house for the market. You may pay more for a written report that will outline everything for you.

Staging fees are billed on a per hour basis or in increments of time, such as a half day or a full day. There are some stagers who charge per square foot just to simplilfy their billing system. If you want a full-service staging job, most professional home stagers will visit with you in your home and conduct a quick tour to determine your needs, then follow up with a quote. Depending on your needs and the factors stated previously, you can expect to pay anywhere from $30 to $75 per hour.

How to Hire a Real Estate Professional

After spending more than 20 years in marketing, design, and home staging, I have acquired a unique insight into selling real estate. Combined with many years of selling and buying property, this has helped me develop my own criteria of what makes a truly effective selling agent in today's real estate market.

Find out who they are

A good real estate agent is involved in the community, networking groups, real estate associations, and most importantly, is a member of the National Association of REALTORS®, who adhere to a strict code of ethics. The fact is, agents sell a great deal of properties to one another so the more people they know the better.

Real estate agents are good listeners, personable, assertive, and confident in their ability to negotiate a good deal on your behalf. They look and act professionally. They are well dressed, respectful, well spoken, and carry themselves with confidence. They are prepared, organized, and enthusiastic about selling your home.

Ask how they will market your property

Before you call to interview a real estate agent, go onto the Internet and "Google" the person (type his or her name into the search window on www.google.com). If the agent has many links show up he or she is an active online marketer. This is essential to selling successfully in today's marketplace.

Advertising in print is proving to be increasingly ineffective, especially magazine advertising, which is only printed once per week. Print advertising in newspapers works well to promote the agent more so than the listing. An agent will usually only advertise in the newspaper because his or her clients believe it to be an effective form of marketing. Home sellers also believe that open houses are a necessity and effective, but most agents acknowledge that they are not very successful in selling homes but, if lucky, can be a great way to meet potential new clients.

It is very important that the agent takes photos seriously. Take a look at his or her current listings and determine if they are impressive. After all, it is the photos that will encourage someone to call to see a property. Are the photos good quality? Is the home well represented? Do they use a wide-angle lens? Are there more than just four photos? Do the images justify the homes' prices?

 The real estate business will always have its up and down cycles. Just remember that while you hear news on a national level, real estate is really very localized. Some communities aren't as affected by the upswings and downturns as others. This holds true even within a city. Do your homework and learn from an area real estate expert.

Kathy Anderson
Ken Meade Realty, AZ

If you are hiring a professional to sell your property, remember that it is in his or her best interest to sell your house for as much money as possible and to keep you happy. Word of mouth will account for 80 percent of the agent's business. When discussing property values, keep in mind that what you see advertised on an MLS website is not necessarily what a house was sold for — so don't let advertised prices affect your expectations for your own property. If your neighbor's house went on the market for $500,000, do not assume that it was a correct assessment value — it could be overpriced. Setting a price that's too high can leave your house on the market for too long, which will leave it stigmatized, as people will wonder what is wrong with the house if it has been on the market for nine months or so.

Every agent should do a thorough market analysis. This involves researching historical data of properties being sold in your neighborhood and surrounding areas. Major components of your property are compared and a deduction is reached after cost allocations for the repairs required for your home.

The agent should also show you the cut sheets (listing information) of the previously sold properties that he or she used to assess the market value of your home, before you sign a contract with him or her. If the agent does not, ask if you can see the cut sheets. If the agent is not prepared to show them to you, consider it a reason for concern. Just be sure to hire a real estate agent you can trust and let the person do what he or she does best: sell real estate.

And, of course, does the agent recognize home staging as one of the most effective marketing tools in selling real estate? If the person doesn't know what home staging is, say, "Thank you for stopping by, I will let you know who I decide to hire." Then hire someone who understands the effectiveness of home staging.

How to Hire a Home Inspector

The following list was composed with the help of Bill Redfern of A Buyer's Choice Home Inspections, to use as a guide for hiring the right professional for your needs. When hiring a home inspector, you must ask the following questions:

- Are you a member, in good standing, of a professional association with a prescribed standard of practice and a code of ethics?

- Are you committed to continuing education?

- Are you insured? (There are many inspectors that are not. You may pay a little less for someone who is uninsured, but it could cost you tens of thousands of dollars if the person misses something significant — and you will have no recourse.)

- Are you able to inspect all areas of concern? (Do not assume that the person does; ask if he or she opens the electrical panel, checks the woodstove/fireplace certification, as well as the attic, on top of the roof or the drainage).

- May I attend the inspection with you? (A good inspector will be happy to have you along and will explain the various problems he or she is finding as you go through the inspection together.)

When will I receive the written report? (Within 24 hours is generally acceptable.)

Is your report typed or handwritten? (This could make a world of difference if you are expected to understand the report.)

After asking these questions, consider whether the person is polite and sounds like someone you could work with. If you have a bad feeling after any of these questions, keep looking for another inspector.

Presale home inspection

Another increasingly popular tool in selling real estate is having your property pre-inspected. I believe in the importance of preinspection and its role in today's real estate market. The benefits are as follows.

Facilitates a faster sale for more money

Having your home pre-inspected before you put it on the market will provide you with a list of repairs and maintenance to work with. If you address the items on this list before calling in your real estate agent, he or she will be able to provide you with a more accurate market analysis. This list will also assist you (and your home stager, if you hire one) in assessing what needs to be done for effective home staging.

Eliminates last-minute collapses in deals or endless renegotiations

There is nothing more frustrating than experiencing the excitement of having sold your house, and then finding out that the deal has fallen through after it was inspected. On top of this, when the buyer hires an inspector, the house is inspected by someone you do not know whose qualifications you are unaware of; regardless, it is the inspector's opinion that buyers will follow. However minor the problems, they will be put on their list of items to use to lower the price of the house. This is where negotiations get pretty tricky. You can either sell the house for less than what you want or the deal will fall through. It can feel like emotional blackmail. All of this can be avoided with a pre-inspection.

Informs you of existing issues

Give yourself the opportunity to address any issues so that you can maintain competitive pricing and protect yourself from over-inflated buyer-procured estimates. Price reductions are typically in increments of $500 or $1000. You may be able to fix a problem and save yourself a lot of money!

Reduces your liability with full disclosure

If you sell your house when major work is required and it is not picked up in a buyer's home inspection, you are likely to be held responsible.

Provides you with the comfort of an unbiased third-party opinion

Particularly for first-time home buyers, a pre-inspection will provide them with peace of mind knowing that they will be buying a house that is well maintained, move-in ready, loved, and worry free.

Helps you avoid future red flags

With a presale inspection, you are able to go through the whole process with the inspector and learn about the various aspects of your home and, most importantly, what work is required to avoid red flags for other home inspections.

What home inspectors look for

It is important that you are aware of the items scrutinized during a home inspection so you are prepared and have an idea of how well your house will stand up to one:

- Roof, vents, flashing, and trim
- Gutters and downspouts
- Skylights, chimneys, and other roof penetrations
- Decks, stoops, porches, walkways, and railings
- Eaves, soffit, and fascia
- Grading and drainage
- Basement, foundation, and crawl space
- Water penetration and foundation movement
- Heating systems
- Cooling systems
- Main water shut-off valves
- Water-heating system
- Interior plumbing fixtures and faucets
- Drainage sump pumps and accessible floats
- Electrical service line and meter box
- Main disconnect and service amperage
- Electrical panels, breakers, fuses, GFCIs, and AFCIs
- Grounding and bonding
- Fireplace damper door and hearth
- Insulation and ventilation
- Garage doors, safety sensors, and openers

Most common defects

As a result of conducting approximately 2 million home inspections system-wide, House-Master franchisers found that more than 40 percent of resale homes on the market, that's two out of every five, will have at least one serious defect when they are listed for sale. The following issues are prominent areas of concern:

- Cracked heat exchanger in furnace
- Failing air-conditioning system
- Environmental hazards, such as radon, water contamination, and asbestos
- Signs of a wet basement
- Defective roofing and/or flashings (or signs of leakage)
- Insect infestation, such as termites or carpenter ants
- Mixed plumbing
- Aluminum wiring
- Horizontal foundation cracks
- Major house settlement
- Undersized electrical system
- Chimney settling, separation, deterioration

What to expect with a home inspection

It is critical to understand what a home inspection is and is not. A home inspection is a visual inspection of how the house is at the time of inspection. It is not intrusive (behind walls) or technically exhaustive. An inspector is not required or expected to move excessive personal belongings for access to any area.

The inspection should provide you with a very thorough report on all visible components of the home and lot. It should point out items due for replacement now or that will be due shortly, for example, safety related hazards such as broken glass, electrical faults, trip and fall hazards, visible mold or mildew or rotting wood.

Finally, you should feel good about your home inspection experience — no matter what is or is not found during the inspection, after completion you should have peace of mind and know much more about your home.

CHAPTER 8

PACKING AND MOVING TIPS

Packing items you will not need in the coming months will make staging, selling, and moving easier. If most of your items are pre-packed, you will have a lot less packing to do after closing the sale and will be able to move relatively quickly. After you move, if you still will not need the pre-packed items for a while, you can always unpack your storage unit or stored boxes when you have the time and energy. In the meantime, you will have everything you need.

Initially, maintaining a staged home may overwhelm some sellers, especially those with young children. Surprisingly, a staged home is much easier to prepare for a showing. The absence of clutter, unnecessary furnishings, and accessories, combined with designated storage boxes in designated areas of the home, leads to a show-ready house in 10 to 15 minutes.

Start Packing!

Moving can be a stressful undertaking, so take advantage of every opportunity to make things easier for yourself. If someone offers to help, give the person the chance to feel good about helping someone who will appreciate it: you. You won't be imposing or owe the person anything, except maybe help when he or she needs it.

Also, treat yourself to "real" boxes and leave searching through the grocery store for discarded boxes to someone else. The luxury of solid, sizable boxes is that they give you peace of mind knowing that they aren't going to collapse and that you can use them after you've unpacked to store items (e.g., winter or summer clothes, holiday decorations, memorabilia).

A "Packing Shopping List" and a "Moving Checklist" are included in Appendix I and on the CD that's included with this book.

The Perfect Packing Practice

If you are using a moving company or enlisting the help of family or friends, they will need to know where everything goes when unloading the truck on moving day and you cannot be everywhere at once to tell them. The following is a system I developed as a result of moving 19 times in 25 years (since moving out of my parents' house) and it works very well for everyone involved.

Before you begin to pack, write a list of rooms and areas to be packed on a piece of paper and assign a colored sticker to each space. Prepare your inventory cards (recipe cards) by placing one of the assigned colored stickers at the top of each card, along with the room name. Use one card for each box that you think you'll need to pack the room. Place the same colored sticker on the box and using your black marker, write the room name on it. As you pack each box, write down the predominate items on its inventory card. At the top of the card, and on the box, write "1 of __." As you continue packing, update the number. For example, if you are onto your second box, you would write "2 of __," then on the next box "3 of __," and so on. When you finish packing the room, you'll know how many boxes were used and you can go back to all the boxes and cards and fill in the total number, such as "1 of 3," "2 of 3," and so on.

For example, Sara's bedroom was assigned a green sticker. So, at the top of each of the three inventory cards and on each of the three boxes, there would be a green sticker with "Sara's bedroom" written next to it. On the first card and the first box, it would also say "1 of 3." The second box and the second card would have green stickers on them, and "Sara's bedroom" and the numbers "2 of 3" would be written on them. Be sure to keep all the cards together and in a location where you can find them easily on moving day.

Arrive ahead of time on moving day and post the colored stickers or coordinating colored paper in each of the rooms, in a place where they can easily be seen. Now when someone comes into the house carrying a box with a green sticker that's marked with "Sara's bedroom," they will know where to take the box and that there should be three that go in that space.

When moving day is over you will know immediately if there are any boxes or items missing, and can then go looking for them or refuse to sign any paperwork if a moving company was responsible. This system is also very useful when storing items to prepare your house for sale. If your belongings are in storage for any length of time, you will forget what was packed in the boxes.

Packing Tips

Here are some general tips to keep in mind while packing:

- This is a great time to rid your home of items you have been holding onto and have not used within the past year. When sorting though your things to pack, classify items into the following three groups:

  - **Donate:** Contact charities in your community to donate your unwanted but still useable items, and arrange for pick-up or delivery.

  - **Pre-pack and store:** These items will include such things as personal decor, seasonal items, and family photos. Store them off-site or in an area of your house that won't be too conspicuous. The bonus in doing this is that it will save you a lot of future stress when your house is sold and you are under a deadline to pack up and move.

- **Sell:** If you choose to sell items, see "How to Have a Successful Yard Sale" in Chapter 5. If you are savvy on the Internet, you can use online auction sites such as eBay, which have proven to be successful tools. Or you can advertise in your local *Buy & Sell* publication.

Pack on a room-by-room basis. Do not mix items from various rooms in one box, with the exception of decor items. Usually wall hangings, pictures, and accessories will not work like they did in your previous home, so it is just easier to keep them all together. After you've unpacked and placed your furnishings, and are ready for finishing touches, all of your decor items will be together.

Pack heavy items in smaller boxes and light items in larger boxes.

Pack your current phone book — in the future you may need to get a hold of residents or businesses in your former hometown.

Records and plates should be packed from left to right, skinny-side down — rather than stacked.

To decrease the chance of breakage, pack items tightly to prevent movement.

Make sure medicine and other toiletries have their lids on securely prior to packing.

If packing by yourself, pack several cartons each day rather than doing it all at once.

Allow children to pack their favorite toys. This gives them a stronger sense of belonging and will help them get used to the idea of moving.

Be cautious with boxes from grocery or liquor stores. They may not be clean and may not have the strength

[Having your home on the market] for any length of time can be stressful. I tell my clients to create seller survival baskets.

One basket can be for all of their daily toiletries they need to get ready in the morning. Stored under the bathroom sink, they can simply throw everything in there when they are done and it's easy to clean up in the mornings.

Another basket can be created with "touch up" cleaning supplies: garbage bags, [cleaners], and other items for those last-minute showings. Grab the supplies for a quick wipe of the counters and bathrooms, throw the daily clutter in the garbage bag (to put away later) and … simple!

Teresa Meyer ASP, IAHSP
Stage a Star Staging & Consulting Services, OH

to withstand the weight of the items you are packing.

- If you are not moving more than approximately 95 miles (150 kilometers), load your plants in the moving truck last, and unload them first. Otherwise, arrange for your plants to be transported directly and independent from your other belongings so they will be available to be watered and taken care of when required.

- Designate one drawer of a dresser for sheets and towels so they will be easily available the first night in your new home

- Remove bulbs from lamps before packing.

- Ask a friend to look after your children and pets when packing and on moving day.

- Keep in mind that professionals may not move the following hazardous materials:
  - Paint
  - Varnish
  - Gasoline
  - Kerosene
  - Oil
  - Bottled gas
  - Aerosol cans
  - Nail polish remover
  - Ammunition
  - Explosives

Make a survival kit

Pack a survival kit that you can take with you in your car or pack last in the moving truck so you can locate it immediately on arrival at the new home. It should include the following:

- **Basic tools:** A hammer, a drill with a wide assortment of bits, a box cutter, and hardware for hanging pictures

- **Bathroom products:** Soap, toilet paper, towels, shampoo, conditioner, and any other personal items required within the next couple of days

- **Kitchen items:** Snacks, drinks, disposable utensils, cups, plates, and paper towels

- **Cleaning products:** Cleaning supplies, and a broom and dustpan

- **Clothing:** Anything you will need for a couple of days, as if you are going away for the weekend

The Big Move
A guide for a stress-free transition

There's more to moving than simply packing your possessions and transporting them to a new location. Moving means great changes in your life: a new home, new friends, new schools, a new job, and possibly a whole new lifestyle.

Such changes can be filled with uncertainty, anxiety, and apprehension. But they can also be exciting and filled with adventure, new opportunities, and chances for personal growth. Although it is not easy to leave a familiar place, consider these tips to help you say good-bye:

- Have a party for the specific purpose of saying good-bye to your friends. Hold it a month or two before your actual move and make it a strictly informal time with an atmosphere that's warm and friendly. This will probably be an emotional time, but it also helps you realize that these people will remain your friends, even though you will be separated by distance.

- Have lunch with old friends and coworkers during the few weeks before your move.

- Plan a backyard barbecue for the neighbors a month before you leave.

- Host a family potluck get-together.

- Take cookies and say good-bye at meetings for your church group, civic organizations, or youth sports teams.

- Your children need their own party to say good-bye to their friends. Let them plan the party, but make sure it is designed to be a light and festive occasion and that it will be something they will look forward to with excitement. It will help them to emotionally prepare for the move.

- Young children may want to take cupcakes, cookies, or fruit and vegetable snacks to school, day care, or a play group.

- Preteens or teens may want to plan their own evening going-away party. Teens may also enjoy treating friends to a day at a local amusement park.

- Plan family outings to say good-bye to your community, by visiting favorite places one last time.

- Have a few nights out at your favorite restaurants, nightspots, or clubs for the purpose of saying good-bye, and, remember, there will be plenty of places in your new community that you'll like equally!

Moving with children

Sooner or later, many families face the prospect of moving. Disruptive as moving can be for parents, the experience can be even more traumatic for children, who may not be a part of the decision to move and may not understand it. Your child may need some time and special attention during the transition. There are some steps you can take to make the entire process less stressful for your entire family.

Many kids thrive on familiarity and routine. As you consider a move, weigh the possible benefits of such a change against your child's need for an environment, school, and social life to which he or she is accustomed.

If your family has recently dealt with a major life change, such as a divorce or death, you may want to postpone a move if possible, to give your child a chance to adjust.

The decision to move may be out of your hands, due to a job transfer or financial issues. Even if you are not happy about the move, try to maintain a positive attitude about it with your child. During times of transition, a parent's moods and attitudes can heavily affect the kids, who may be looking for reassurance.

Discussing the move with your child

No matter what the circumstances, the most important way you can prepare your child is to talk about the move early on and often.

It is a good idea to give your child as much information about the move as you can, as soon as possible. Answer your child's questions completely and truthfully, and be receptive to both positive and negative reactions. Even if the move means a clear improvement in family life, your child may not understand that, and he or she may be focused on the frightening aspects of the change.

Involve your child in the planning process as much as possible. If your child feels like a participant in the house-hunting process or the search for a new school, the change may feel less like it is being forced on him or her.

If you are moving across town, you may want to take your child to visit the new house (or see it being built) and explore the new neighborhood. If distance prevents this, provide as much information as you can about the new home, city, state, province, or country. If you cannot do so yourself, a relative or friend may be able to take pictures of the new house and your child's new school. A real estate agent may even be willing to do this. Be sure to learn about where your child can do any favorite activities in the new location.

Moving with babies, toddlers, and preschoolers

Children who are younger than the age of six may be the easiest to move, as they have a limited capacity to understand the changes the move will involve. However, your guidance is still crucial. Here are some steps you can take to ease the transition for your child:

- Keep explanations clear and simple.

- Use a story to explain the move or use toy trucks and furniture to act it out.

- When you pack your toddler's toys in boxes, make sure you explain that you aren't throwing them away.

- If your new home is nearby and vacant, take your child to see it before the move and take a few toys over each time.

- Hold off on getting rid of your child's old bedroom furniture, which may provide a sense of comfort in the new house.

- Avoid making other big changes during the move, such as toilet training or advancing a toddler to a bed from a crib.

- Arrange for your toddler or preschooler to stay with a babysitter on moving day.

Moving with school-age children

A child in elementary school may be relatively open to the idea of a move. But your child will still need serious consideration and your help throughout the transition.

There are generally two schools of thought about "the right time to move." Some experts say that summer is the best time, to avoid disrupting the school year. Others say that mid year is a better time, so a child can meet other kids right away.

To avoid any glitches that would add stress to your child, it is a good idea to gather any information the new school will need to process the transfer. That may include the most recent report card or transcript, birth certificate, or medical records.

Moving with teens

It is not uncommon for teens to actively rebel against a move. Your teen has probably invested considerable energy in a particular social group and may be involved in a romantic relationship. Your family's move may mean that your teen has to miss a long-awaited event, such as a prom.

It is particularly important to let your teen known that you want to hear about any concerns and that you respect those concerns. Blanket assurances may seem to your teen like you are dismissing his or her feelings. It may help to explain to your teen that the move is a type of rehearsal for future changes, for example, college or a new job.

You may want to begin planning a trip back to the neighborhood after the move, if that's possible.

If your teen remains strongly resistant to the move, you might want to consider letting him or her stay in the old location with a friend or relative, if you have that option. This may be particularly helpful if you are moving partway through the school year.

After moving with children

After the move, it is a good idea to get your child's room in order before turning your attention to the rest of the house. Also, try to maintain your regular schedule for meals and bedtime to provide a sense of familiarity for your child.

When your child does start school, you may want to go along to meet as many teachers as possible and ask to introduce your child to the principal. Set realistic expectations about your child's transition. Generally, teachers expect new kids to feel somewhat comfortable in their classes in about six weeks. Some kids may take less time, whereas some may need more. After a while, if you are still concerned about your child's transition, a family therapist may be able to provide some helpful guidance.

A move can present many challenges, but many good things can also come from this kind of change. Your family may grow closer, and you may learn more about your child by going through this experience together.

Moving with pets

The process of moving can be stressful for all family members, both people and pets. The Humane Society in the United States, or the SPCA in Canada, can offer you safety guidelines to keep in mind while moving so the experience will be less stressful for the entire family. The following are some tips you should keep in mind before, during, and after your move.

Before you move

- Familiarize yourself with the local pet ordinances of the area where you'll be moving. Each community has a unique set of laws, usually including things such as licensing, leashing, and vaccination, but occasionally there are also restrictions on the number of pets a person can have in a household without a special permit.

- Visit your veterinarian. Depending on the location of your new home, your pet might need additional vaccinations or health certificates. It is also a good idea to discuss whether or not your pet will need medication to help calm him or her during the moving process.

- Maintain your pet's routine. Like people, pets are often disturbed by the stir that is caused by moving. During the weeks prior to the move, be sure that you keep your pet's walking, playing, and eating times as regular as possible so that he or she can feel less confused about the change.

- Prepare your pet's ID tag. Purchase an ID tag with your new address and phone number(s) as soon as you know your new contact information. An up-to-date ID tag is the best way for you to ensure that you will be reunited with your pet in the unfortunate case that he or she becomes separated from you during the moving commotion.

- Invest in a high-quality, sturdy pet carrier or seatbelt harness. Allow your pet to gradually get used to spending time in the carrier or wearing the harness. Placing your pet's blanket or favorite toy inside of the carrier might help your pet feel more relaxed.

Keep pets safe while you move

- Practice moving day security. While furniture is being moved out, confine your pet to a safe, quiet space (such as a bathroom) so that your pet cannot escape. Place a large "DO NOT ENTER" sign on the door, and let everyone involved in the move know that the room is off-limits.

- Ensure a safe car trip. Make frequent stops, and always use a leash while you are walking your dog at rest stops. For everyone's safety, make sure to use a well-ventilated and securely placed pet carrier. Otherwise, make sure that your pet is secured by a pet safety harness. Never leave pets alone in a parked vehicle. During warm weather the temperature in a car can rise to 120 degrees in a matter of minutes, even with the windows slightly open.

- Keep a pet travel kit with you. While on the road be sure to pack more food, medications, and water than you may need. Having extra food that is familiar will help to avoid stomach upsets should your trip take longer than planned. Be sure to bring along a scooper and plastic bags to clean up after you walk your dog.

- Stay in hotels that accept pets and do not travel with your pet on an airplane unless it is absolutely necessary. For more information and for tips on airplane safety for pets, talk to the Humane Society (in the US) or the SPCA (in Canada).

What to do with your pet after you move

Introduce your pet to your new home.

- Keep your pet confined in a secure room while furniture is being moved in. Comfort your pet with his or her familiar blankets, toys, and food and water while secured in the room. After the hustle and bustle of the move has died down, allow your pet to explore his or her new home with you. Placing items such as your pet's favorite food bowl, bed, toys, and litter box in their new locations will help the pet become comfortable with his or her new surroundings.

- Remove odors from previous pets. Moving into a home in which other pets have previously resided might encourage your pet to mark his or her territory.

CHAPTER 9

THE NEW FIRST IMPRESSION

Now that your house is staged, remember that photographs are the new first impression. Although curb appeal is still very important, photographs posted on the Internet will make or break any chance your property has to make the list of houses for potential buyers to consider.

An astounding 84 percent of people conduct research on the Internet when looking to buy a house. It is important that you know how to take great photographs, so I've enlisted the help of professional photographer Tara Gillis, to provide you with tips from both of our points of view. You will benefit from both professions to help capture real estate photos that will impress your online visitors.

How to Take Great Photographs

Remember, everything takes time to learn! Photography is a skill and you do not become a photographer after purchasing a camera. After reading these tips and techniques, you will be one step closer.

Equipment

If you are in the market for a new camera, the best one to buy to take great photographs is a digital SLR camera with a wide-angle lens. It is your best option if you want interchangeable lenses and the benefit of seeing images immediately after taking the shot. There are many options and prices available when buying a camera. If you are not sure what to buy, ask the staff at your local camera store. They will be able to guide you through your purchase based on your photographic needs. That being said, not all is lost if you already own a camera that does not have a wide-angle lens. Adequate photos could be taken even with a Polaroid from the '70s if the tips provided are followed.

Having a tripod will prevent the camera from shaking, which is essential if you want to use manual settings on your camera. A tripod can be purchased at your local camera supply store and is often quite inexpensive. It will also allow you to let go of the camera and use the self-timer so you don't move the camera during exposure.

Get to know your camera

If you are unsure of how to make the most of your camera settings, consider taking a night class at your local community college, ask a professional to give you a few lessons, or join a camera club in your community. Also be sure to read the manual that comes with your camera. The better you know how it works, the more time you can spend shooting and the less time you will spend being frustrated.

Experiment with your camera. For those of you who are more familiar with the manual settings on your camera, try a longer shutter speed and change the ISO and the aperture. Every change will give you a slightly different result. Note what happens with each change and you are well on your way to taking better images. Take a few pictures with each setting and refocus each time, as a sharp image is imperative to great photography.

Wide-angle lenses

If buying a new camera, be sure that whichever one you decide to purchase has a wide-angle lens. If you are not an avid photographer, there are still a variety of "point and shoot" cameras on the market that have built-in automatic-focus features and wide-angle lenses. It makes a dramatic difference in what you can capture in a photograph, especially in small spaces such as bathrooms, small bedrooms, and kitchens.

With a wide-angle lens you will no longer be capturing half of what you intend to include in a photo. After using the camera for your immediate real estate needs, a wide-angle lens will help you capture holiday photos that will include all of your family members so nobody gets their feelings hurt.

To see the difference this lens makes, see the sample photos of an extremely small room taken with and without a wide-angle lens on the CD, under **Wide-angle**.

Focal point

Locate the focal point in the room then select the most interesting portion of the room that highlights that feature. Figure out the best angle, shoot from the corner of the room, and try all the corners. What may seem like the best angle initially may not always yield the best image.

Lighting

Experiment with the light by shooting at different times of the day. A nice stream of sunlight often looks beautiful, but can be very harsh on camera. Use natural light as much as you can. If you find the sun is too harsh, put a sheer panel in front of the window to diffuse the light; it acts as a giant soft box (a professional light diffuser) and gives a nice glow to the room. Overcast skies are often the perfect weather for shooting interiors: The windows look bright but the light doesn't cast harsh shadows. Add a few lamps or light sources in the background if the room is a bit darker than you'd like. Lighting is the most important factor in creating great imagery.

Manipulate contrasting elements

Look for opportunities to use contrasting elements to your advantage. A bright vase of flowers or decor placed on or near a focal point will help guide the viewer's eye to that object. A table lamp that is turned on will cast warm light and often the eye will go to that light first. For example, if you want a fireplace to be the focal point in your photograph, place lit candles on the mantle on both sides of a wall hanging. After taking the photo, your eye should immediately find the candlelight and then the focus point: the fireplace.

Portrait or landscape

In reference to print, the term "portrait" is used to indicate that a photograph's height is greater than its width. In other words, the photo was taken vertically. "Landscape" refers to a photograph that is wider than it is tall, which means that it was taken horizontally. Most interior photos are landscape shots, but smaller spaces such as small bedrooms and bathrooms may require you to take a portrait shot. However, if you have a wide-angle lens, you may be able to capture the whole bathroom in a landscape shot.

Don't show off your ceiling

Every room in every property has various layouts and design concepts that make each house unique. Rooms will have various features that you will want to highlight in your photos to attract potential buyers on the Internet.

However, one feature that you can be sure every house has is a ceiling. This is not something you need to show in your photos. This is a common mistake made in real estate photos. The photo in this example uses one-third of the composition on the ceiling! Always remember to do a final check on the composition of your photos before taking them. Look at the ceiling line to make sure that it is close to the top of your viewfinder in the camera. See this photo example on the CD, named **CEILING**.

Mirror, mirror on the wall

When taking pictures of a bathroom or a room where there is a mirror, keep an eye on your position in the room. Capturing the photographer in a real estate photo is distracting and looks unprofessional.

Distraction

Equally distracting is when people or pets are caught in the background. It also looks especially unprofessional in a real estate photo. Avoid photographing letters or numbers in a room; they draw the eye to them and can often become the focus of your image.

Hot spots

Be aware of reflective surfaces in your shot, such as shiny metals or mirrors. Light will bounce off of these areas and back into the camera creating a hot spot, which will show up as white spots on your photo. See the example photo on the CD, named **Hotspots**.

Trick the camera

When taking photos in a room with a window on a sunny day, you will need to "trick" the camera if you are using the auto function on a digital camera. Taking a picture in this condition will not give you the results you need for a good real estate shot; your photo will have extreme bright and dark areas.

To "trick" the camera, look through your viewfinder and determine the brightest area and the darkest area of what you want to capture in your photo. Now pick a point between those two extremes and position your camera as if you are going to take a picture of that area. You will see the camera come into focus and adjust the lighting to accommodate it. Now hold the shutter button down halfway to "lock in" the shutter. Turn your camera back to what you want captured in your photo and take the picture. Essentially, you will have tricked your camera into taking the photo without the extreme bright and dark areas that would have resulted had you simply taken the shot. A great example of this can be found on the CD, in the photos under **Trick**.

Make it straight

Make sure the camera is straight, not inclining up or down and not tilted to either side. Look for something vertical in your shot, such as a wall, a desk, or a mirror. Align the inside of the viewfinder with one of these vertical points and your camera will produce a photo that looks and feels natural.

Prepare Your Photos for the Internet

People who spend a lot of time on the Internet do not have much patience when it comes to download time (which is how long it takes for the page to show up on the screen). If you are not familiar with the online world, you need to be aware that pages are expected to show up immediately and that potential buyers will not spend time waiting for a photo to show up. Text will download first because text files are smaller, but photos are larger files of information that can take much longer. Ideally you should keep your photo files smaller than 25 kilobytes (kb), and they should never be higher than 50 kb to ensure a quick download speed.

Most digital camera default settings create fairly large file sizes. Check the instruction booklet that comes with your camera to see how you can adjust the DPI (Dots Per Inch, which determines the quality of a photo) to the lowest setting. Ideally you should take your photos at 72 or 96 DPI, which is the standard online photo file size.

You can also change a picture's size after you take it, by opening it in any photo software and reducing the DPI there. There are many user-friendly photo software packages on the market today that are economical and come with preset functions for preparing photos for the Internet.

Also, crop your photo to remove any unwanted areas and maximize the quality of the layout in your photo. Whatever you do, do not overwrite the original photo file. After making your changes, do a "Save as" so as to avoid making that mistake; if you simply hit "Save," there is no going back. The picture size for the

Internet may look good onscreen, but if you try to print the photo, it will show up very tiny.

Make photos count

It took me less than a minute to find a common bedroom photo on the Internet real estate pages. These kinds of photos are great examples of why staging a room to sell lifestyle is an essential part of preparing photos for the Internet. Often the pictures have very little purpose, and set up poor expectations with potential buyers. The images can give a dismal implication of what is to be seen if someone arranges to view the home, even if it is a beautiful house in the upper end of the housing market. These photos will turn away potential buyers. See the photo named **Make Photos Count** on the CD for an example.

Watch what you say online

As the old saying goes, "A picture says a thousand words." I have found photos online that say, "This house stinks with cigarette smoke, has nicotine on the walls, has problems with insects, and has limited storage." These photos will turn away potential buyers. See an example photo on the CD, named **Online**.

Where to post your listing

Just to be clear, I have not used many of the websites I have listed on the CD in the "Resources" file. They are simply suggestions of places to explore to find out how you can maximize your online exposure.

That being said, I am thoroughly impressed with what Point2Agent (http://agent.point2.com) has to offer, primarily because it is the real estate industry's largest syndication network. If you have your listing posted on this site, you or your real estate agent can also have it posted on the many other websites that work with this site, including other agents' websites, anywhere in the world.

Although having a real estate agent still proves to be one of the most effective ways to sell your home, you are not restricted to that route. You can still do your own online marketing and submit your house to many of the most popular real estate websites, with the exception of MLS and the one-stop marketing machine Point2NLS. However, you can still submit to their partners individually, some of which are free (but many do charge fees).

EFFECTIVE SIGN DESIGNS

FURNITURE LAYOUT GRID
(FOR EFFECTIVE TRAFFIC FLOW)

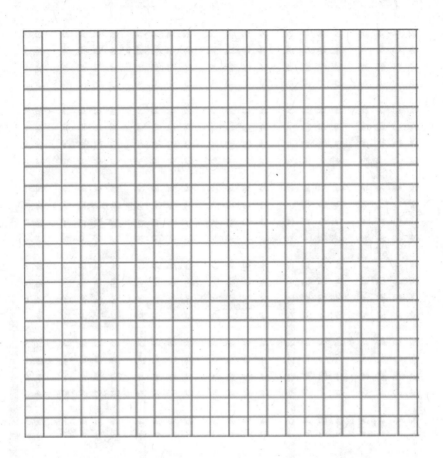

MASTER TO-DO LIST

List items to change, fix, organize, etc.:
1.
2.
3.
4.
5.
6.
7.
8.
9.
10.
11.
12.
13.
14.
15.
16.
17.
18.
19.
20.

MOVING CHECKLIST

Careful organization and forward planning can minimize the stress of moving. Use the "Moving Checklist" in conjunction with the "Who to Notify Checklist" to guide you through the six weeks leading up to moving day.

Six weeks before the move	☒	Date:
Confirm the date of your move.	☐	
If you are currently renting, notify your landlord of your moving date.	☐	
Check your home insurance to make sure you have coverage from the day you move into your new home.	☐	
If you are using professional movers, obtain written quotes from several moving companies. Get references and check the limits of their insurance.	☐	
If you are not using professional movers, arrange for friends to help.	☐	
Book extra storage space if required.	☐	
Notify the relevant utility companies of your departure.	☐	
Start getting rid of possessions you no longer need. Decide which items can be taken to a charity shop, sold at a yard sale, or offered to your friends.	☐	
If you need new furniture or carpets, order them now and arrange delivery for when you move in.	☐	
Two weeks before the move	☒	**Date:**
Start packing nonessential items such as books and out-of-season clothes into boxes.	☐	
De-register from your doctor, dentist, and optician if you are moving out of the area.	☐	
Visit the post office and arrange for your mail to be forwarded (you will be charged a fee for this service).	☐	
Notify other regular delivery services (such as for newspapers) that you'll be moving and give them a date you want the service to stop.	☐	
If you have children or pets, arrange for someone to look after them during the move.	☐	

Make a list of everyone who should know about the move. Send out "change of address" cards or emails.	☐	
Finalize arrangements with your moving company. Confirm arrival times and make sure your movers have directions to your current and your new address.	☐	
Arrange a time to collect the keys for your new home from the real estate agent.	☐	
Notify the bank of any changes to direct debits and/or standing orders.	☐	

OPEN HOUSE CHECKLIST

KITCHEN/DINING ROOM

☐ Sinks, faucets, and all reflective items are glistening.

☐ All exposed appliances are clean inside and out.

☐ Contents in the refrigerator and cupboards are minimal and tidy.

☐ Countertops and tables are clear of everything, with the exception of a display item such as a bowl of fruit on the counter and/or a flower arrangement on the table.

☐ Pet dishes are put under the sink.

☐ Dirty dishes are cleaned and put away into cupboards.

☐ Garbage and compost are emptied and containers are out of sight.

☐ Knives and sharp objects are hidden.

LIVING ROOM

☐ Windows are glistening.

☐ All items with the exception of designated display items are hidden.

☐ All surfaces are free of dust and fingerprints.

☐ Floor is clean.

☐ Soft music is playing.

☐ The fireplace is lit/on.

BEDROOM(S)

☐ All clean clothes are put away and dirty laundry is stored in the washer, or in a decorative laundry basket with a lid to hide contents.

☐ The bed is dressed in luxurious linen, turned down neatly, and plush with pillows.

☐ All personal items used daily are hidden in containers and/or stored under the bed.

☐ The closet is neat.

BATHROOM(S)

☐ The toilet seat is down.

☐ Everything is spotless and shining.

☐ Trash bin is empty and tucked away under sink.

☐ Personal items from the shower and counter are tucked away in baskets and stored under the sink.

☐ Shower curtain is one-third open.

CURB APPEAL

☐ Lawn is mowed and watered.

☐ Property is clear of trash and animal droppings.

☐ Toys and other items are stored away.

☐ Walkways, porches, and decks are clean.

☐ The driveway is empty to allow potential buyers to park.

ENTRANCEWAY

☐ There are *no* odors, such as from pets, children, smoking, etc.

☐ The area and all doorknobs are clean.

☐ All boots, shoes, coats, hats, and "drop off" items are removed from the area.

GENERALLY

☐ Every light for every showing is turned on, even during the day.

☐ The house is approximately 72 degrees Fahrenheit (°F) or 21 degrees Celsius (°C).

☐ All garbage containers are empty and the outside of the property is clear.

☐ Pets are staying somewhere else and all their supplies are tucked away.

☐ No one is home for open houses or showings.

☐ Soft relaxing music is on (preferably throughout house, if not, then at least in the living room and master bedroom).

- [ ] All ash catchers such as ashtrays and incense burners are removed from every room.
- [ ] Flooring in every room is freshly vacuumed (cleaned if hardwood).
- [ ] All surfaces are dusted; windows, walls, and doors are clean of any fingerprints.
- [ ] All remaining window coverings are open as wide as they can be (if the view is becoming and not unsightly).
- [ ] _____
- [ ] _____
- [ ] _____
- [ ] _____
- [ ] _____
- [ ] _____
- [ ] _____

PACKING SHOPPING LIST

☐ **Small, medium, and large boxes.** Use small boxes for heavy items such as books, CDs; medium boxes for typical items; and large boxes for light items such as linen, clothing, pillows, lampshades, etc.

☐ **Six-packs of clear packing tape (at least two).** There is nothing more frustrating than running out of tape and having to run to the store to get more, especially when you do not live near one that sells it. It is cheaper to purchase tape in six packs; you'll always use any extra in your new home and if you are anything like me, you will need to have a roll of tape in every room because you will keep misplacing it.

☐ **Two black markers.** Use markers to write on the outside of the boxes to identify which room it should go into. Words should be easy to read when trying to identify where it should go when it's being moved. It can be pretty frustrating for those helping to try and read words written with a fine pen.

☐ **Recipe cards for your "inventory."** These will be useful to help you to find your belongings when they are packed. You will know where to find everything even if boxes have been placed in the wrong area.

☐ **Various colored stickers.** Use these to create a quick reference to which room an item should be placed when your belongings are being moved.

WHO TO NOTIFY CHECKLIST

Service and Utility Companies	☒	Date:
Water	☐	
Gas/Oil/Propane/Natural Gas	☐	
Electricity/Hydro	☐	
Telephone	☐	
Internet Provider	☐	
Cell Phone	☐	
Post Office	☐	
Cable/Satellite Provider	☐	
Video Rental Companies	☐	
Security	☐	
Financial	☒	**Date:**
Banks	☐	
Building Societies	☐	
Credit Cards	☐	
City or Council Tax Department	☐	
Investments	☐	
Employer(s)	☐	
Insurance	☐	
Pension	☐	
Government Tax Revenue/Agency	☐	
Social Security/Social Insurance	☐	
Lawyer	☐	

Health	☒	Date:
Doctor	☐	
Dentist	☐	
Optician	☐	
Insurance	☐	

Motoring	☒	Date:
Vehicle Registration	☐	☐
Vehicle Insurance	☐	☐
Breakdown Recovery Company (e.g., AAA or CAA)	☐	☐
Department of Motor Vehicles (where applicable)	☐	☐

Others	☒	Date:
Friends and Relatives	☐	
Subscriptions	☐	
Clubs	☐	
Library	☐	
Schools/Colleges	☐	

APPENDIX II — HOME IMPROVEMENT CHECKLISTS

BASEMENT IMPROVEMENTS CHECKLIST

- [ ] Remove wallpaper and/or borders.
- [ ] Repair nail holes, cracks, and stains in Gyproc, and repaint walls, if necessary.
- [ ] Fix cracks in foundation, floors, and ceiling.
- [ ] Paint or replace trim and baseboards if dated, worn, or damaged.
- [ ] Change or fix all doors and windows that do not operate effortlessly, or make unnecessary noise.
- [ ] Change or fix furnaces, water heaters, and/or other household appliances not in good repair.
- [ ] Fix blocked drains.
- [ ] Change or fix light fixtures that do not work, are dated, or are not to scale with surroundings.
- [ ] Change lightbulbs to those with maximum wattage.

Notes:

BATHROOM IMPROVEMENTS CHECKLIST

☐ Remove wallpaper and/or borders.

☐ Repair nail holes, cracks, and stains in Gyproc, and repaint walls, if necessary.

☐ Change or fix faucets and fixtures that are chipped, tarnished, worn, or outdated.

☐ Change or fix broken, cracked, or stained toilet seats or hinges.

☐ Change or fix bathtub if it is worn, chipped, or damaged.

☐ Change or fix dated, damaged, or worn flooring. Replace any carpet with water-resistant flooring.

☐ Change or fix any plumbing that leaks.

☐ Fix caulking around bathtub or sink.

☐ Change or fix all doors and windows that do not operate effortlessly, or make unnecessary noise.

☐ Change or fix light fixtures that do not work, are dated, or are not to scale with surroundings.

☐ Change lightbulbs to those with maximum wattage.

☐ Replace any shower curtain that cannot be cleaned until it looks new.

☐ Replace bar soap with a bottle of liquid soap.

Notes:

BEDROOM IMPROVEMENTS CHECKLIST

- ☐ Remove wallpaper and/or borders.
- ☐ Repair nail holes, cracks, and stains in Gyproc, and repaint walls, if necessary.
- ☐ Paint or replace trim and baseboards if dated, worn, or damaged.
- ☐ Change or fix all doors and windows that do not operate effortlessly, or make unnecessary noise.
- ☐ Repair any damage to windows, windowsills, floors and/or ceiling.
- ☐ Get carpets professionally cleaned, or replace them if dated, worn, or damaged.
- ☐ Replace any linen not lending itself to a luxuriously displayed bed.
- ☐ Change or fix light fixtures that do not work, are dated, or are not to scale with surroundings.
- ☐ Change lightbulbs to those with maximum wattage.

_____

Notes

CLOSETS AND LINEN SPACE
IMPROVEMENTS CHECKLIST

☐ Repaint tired or dented walls and shelving.

☐ Fix or replace any broken hardware or shelving.

☐ Change or fix all doors that do not operate effortlessly, or make unnecessary noise.

☐ Install a closet organizer; a big impression for space seekers.

☐ Change lightbulbs to those with maximum wattage.

Notes:

CURB APPEAL IMPROVEMENTS CHECKLIST

- [ ] Reconsider your exterior color scheme if you have more than three colors on your home, unless it is a Victorian style.

- [ ] Repair and reseal driveway if it looks damaged and/or worn, or ensure gravel driveway is raked and consistent.

- [ ] Repair cracked walkways if damaged or not kept in good repair.

- [ ] Paint or replace wood trim or edging if tattered and/or damaged.

- [ ] Fix broken fences and paint them, if worn and/or chipped.

- [ ] Clean, stain, water-seal, and/or paint all wood decking.

- [ ] Fix or change damaged or compromised window frames, or windows with broken seals.

- [ ] Fix or paint garage doors if broken or in need of paint.

- [ ] Paint front door and trim if it is tired or chipped. Consider painting the front door with a complementary but different color from the rest of the house to create a lasting impression. Your eye should immediately find the front door upon arrival.

- [ ] Update doorbells, house numbers, knockers; they should be coordinated and appear new, not tarnished.

- [ ] Consider front door accessories such as a kick plate, new hardware, or trim, which can add excitement (much like jewelry on a plain black suit).

- [ ] Fix sticky door handles or locks (they make it difficult to enter and do not make a good first impression).

- [ ] Clean or fix gutters and downspouts.

- [ ] Change or fix light fixtures that do not work, are dated, or are not to scale with surroundings.

- [ ] Change lightbulbs in exterior fixtures to those with maximum wattage.

Notes:

DINING ROOM IMPROVEMENTS CHECKLIST

☐ Remove wallpaper and/or borders.

☐ Repair nail holes, cracks, and stains in Gyproc, and repaint walls if necessary.

☐ Replace and/or paint windowsills, trim, and baseboards if dated, worn, or damaged.

☐ Change or fix all doors and windows that do not operate effortlessly, or make unnecessary noise.

☐ Repair damage to windows, floors, and/or ceiling.

☐ Get flooring or carpets professionally cleaned, or replace if dated, worn, or damaged.

☐ Resurface wood floors if worn or damaged.

☐ Change or fix light fixtures that do not work, are dated, or are not to scale with surroundings.

☐ Change lightbulbs to those with maximum wattage.

Notes:

FAMILY OR GREAT ROOM
IMPROVEMENTS CHECKLIST

☐ Remove wallpaper and/or borders.

☐ Repair nail holes, cracks, and stains in Gyproc, and repaint walls if necessary.

☐ Paint or replace trim and baseboards if dated, worn, or damaged.

☐ Change or fix all doors and windows that do not operate effortlessly, or make unnecessary noise.

☐ Get carpets professionally cleaned, or replace if dated, worn, or damaged.

☐ Change or fix light fixtures that do not work, are dated, or are not to scale with surroundings.

☐ Change lightbulbs to those with maximum wattage.

Notes:

FRONT ENTRANCE IMPROVEMENTS CHECKLIST

- ☐ Remove wallpaper and/or borders.

- ☐ Repair nail holes, cracks, and stains in Gyproc, and repaint walls if necessary.

- ☐ Repair any damage to windows, windowsills, floors, and/or ceiling.

- ☐ Paint or replace trim and baseboards if dated, worn, or damaged.

- ☐ Get carpets professionally cleaned, or replace if dated, worn, or damaged.

- ☐ Change or fix all doors and windows that do not operate effortlessly, or make unnecessary noise.

- ☐ Change or fix light fixtures that do not work, are dated, or are not to scale with surroundings.

- ☐ Change lightbulbs to those with maximum wattage.

Notes:

GARAGE IMPROVEMENTS CHECKLIST

☐ Make sure garage door opener works.

☐ Change or fix any door hardware that is old, worn, or not functioning properly.

☐ Change or fix all doors and windows that do not operate effortlessly, or make unnecessary noise.

☐ Paint and grease garage door.

☐ Repair walls that are damaged.

☐ Repaint walls, doors, floor, window frames, and/or wood trim that cannot be scrubbed clean.

☐ Change or fix light fixtures that do not work, are dated, or are not to scale with surroundings.

☐ Change lightbulbs to those with maximum wattage.

Notes:

HALLWAYS/STAIRWAYS
IMPROVEMENTS CHECKLIST

☐ Remove wallpaper and/or borders.

☐ Repair nail holes, cracks, and stains in Gyproc, and repaint walls, if necessary. Repair any damage to floors and/or ceiling.

☐ Paint or replace trim and baseboards, if dated, worn, or damaged.

☐ Change or fix all doors and windows that do not operate effortlessly, or make unnecessary noise.

☐ Get carpets professionally cleaned, or replace them if dated, worn, or damaged.

☐ Change or fix light fixtures that do not work, are dated, or are not to scale with surroundings.

☐ Change lightbulbs to those with maximum wattage.

Notes:

KITCHEN IMPROVEMENTS CHECKLIST

☐ Remove wallpaper and/or borders.

☐ Repair nail holes, cracks, and stains in Gyproc, and repaint walls if necessary.

☐ Paint or replace trim and baseboards if dated, worn, or damaged.

☐ Change or fix damaged or worn cupboard doors.

☐ Change or fix hinges and/or cupboard hardware.

☐ Change or fix leaky and/or loose faucets.

☐ Change or fix dated or damaged countertops.

☐ Change or fix all doors and windows that do not operate effortlessly, or make unnecessary noise.

☐ Change or fix exhaust fans that do not operate properly or are noisy.

☐ Change or clean filters in range hoods.

☐ Change or fix light fixtures that do not work, are dated, or are not to scale with surroundings.

☐ Change lightbulbs to those with maximum wattage.

Notes:

LAUNDRY ROOM IMPROVEMENTS CHECKLIST

☐ Remove wallpaper and/or borders.

☐ Repair nail holes, cracks, and stains in Gyproc, and repaint walls, if necessary.

☐ Change or fix all doors and windows that do not operate effortlessly, or make unnecessary noise.

☐ Change or fix wood trim or baseboards that may be damaged and/or worn.

☐ Repair any broken shelving.

☐ Change or fix any laundry appliances that are not in good repair.

☐ Change or fix light fixtures that do not work, are dated, or are not to scale with surroundings.

☐ Change lightbulbs to those with maximum wattage.

Notes:

LIVING ROOM IMPROVEMENTS CHECKLIST

☐ Remove wallpaper and/or borders.

☐ Repair nail holes, cracks, and stains in Gyproc, and repaint walls, if necessary.

☐ Repair damage to windows, windowsills, floors, and/or ceiling.

☐ Replace and/or paint windowsills, trim, and baseboards, if dated, worn, or damaged.

☐ Get carpets professionally cleaned, or replace if dated, worn, or damaged. Resurface wood floors if worn or damaged.

☐ Change or fix all doors and windows that do not operate effortlessly, or make unnecessary noise.

☐ Change or fix light fixtures that do not work, are dated, or are not to scale with surroundings.

☐ Change lightbulbs to those with maximum wattage

Notes:

OFFICE IMPROVEMENTS CHECKLIST

- ☐ Remove wallpaper and/or borders.
- ☐ Repair nail holes, cracks, and stains in Gyproc, and repaint walls, if necessary.
- ☐ Repair damage to floors and/or ceiling.
- ☐ Paint or replace trim and baseboards if dated, worn, or damaged.
- ☐ Get carpets professionally cleaned, or replace if dated, worn, or damaged.
- ☐ Change or fix all doors and windows that do not operate effortlessly, or make unnecessary noise.
- ☐ Change or fix light fixtures that do not work, are dated, or are not to scale with surroundings.
- ☐ Change lightbulbs to those with maximum wattage.

Notes:

REC ROOM/GAMES ROOM
IMPROVEMENTS CHECKLIST

☐ Remove wallpaper and/or borders.

☐ Repair nail holes, cracks, and stains in Gyproc, and repaint walls if necessary.

☐ Repair damage to floors and/or ceiling.

☐ Paint or replace trim and baseboards if dated, worn, or damaged.

☐ Get carpets professionally cleaned, or replace if dated, worn, or damaged.

☐ Change or fix all doors and windows that do not operate effortlessly, or make unnecessary noise.

☐ Change or fix light fixtures that do not work, are dated, or are not to scale with surroundings.

☐ Change lightbulbs to those with maximum wattage.

Notes:

YARD IMPROVEMENTS CHECKLIST

- ☐ Change or fix hardware on fence door/gate.
- ☐ Fix or paint broken fences, if worn and/or chipped.
- ☐ Fix walkways and/or patio stones (if cracked, damaged, or not kept in good repair).
- ☐ Weed and mulch gardens.
- ☐ Change or fix windows with broken seals, and damaged or compromised window frames.
- ☐ Change or fix wood trim or edging that is tattered and/or damaged.
- ☐ Clean, stain, water seal, and/or paint all wood decking.
- ☐ Change or fix light fixtures that do not work, are dated, or are not to scale with surroundings.
- ☐ Change lightbulbs to those with maximum wattage.

Notes:

BASEMENT STAGING CHECKLIST

PAY ATTENTION TO THE DETAILS:

☐ Sweep, vacuum, and clean floors.

☐ Clean walls, light switches, fixtures, hardware, windows, casings, baseboards, and trim.

☐ Clean fireplace or woodstove.

☐ Clean furnaces, hot water heaters, and other appliances so they appear as new as possible.

☐ Clean any signs of mold or mildew.

☐ Remove any sign of insects.

☐ Find and arrange furnishings to reflect a lifestyle of leisure (if basement is finished).

☐ Ensure that areas around walls and items of interest are available for inspection.

☐ Turn on heat in the winter months.

☐ Bring in a dehumidifier and/or an ozone machine to rid dampness and odors.

SELL, DONATE, OR STORE:

☐ "When I get around to it" items and projects.

☐ Items that were to be sorted from the last move.

☐ Sports and leisure items you thought you would use but haven't in the last year.

Notes:

SELF-COUNSEL PRESS — DO YOUR OWN HOME STAGING – AIII-1 08

BATHROOM STAGING CHECKLIST

PAY ATTENTION TO THE DETAILS:

- [ ] Clean walls and floors.
- [ ] Clean all countertops and surfaces.
- [ ] Clean the toilet, sink, tub, and/or shower.
- [ ] Clean shower curtain or doors and ensure there is no sign of soap residue.
- [ ] Ensure windows, mirrors, fixtures, chrome, and brass fixtures glisten.
- [ ] Ensure grout is like new.
- [ ] Eliminate any rust from shower and/or tub and sinks.
- [ ] Display window coverings if required.
- [ ] Display fresh flowers in a vase on the counter.
- [ ] Display shower and/or tub by opening the curtain or shower doors by one-third.
- [ ] Display a set of luxurious towels (to be used specifically for open houses and/or showings).
- [ ] Keep the toilet seat down (very important).
- [ ] Ensure there are no odors.

SELL, DONATE, OR STORE:

- [ ] Decorative rugs and covers.
- [ ] Non-matching and/or extra towels.
- [ ] Personal things and those things you need daily (store in baskets and place under the sink or in a cabinet).
- [ ] Trash cans, cleaning products, and plunger (place under the sink or elsewhere).
- [ ] Reading material (place in a magazine rack or elsewhere).

Notes:

BEDROOM STAGING CHECKLIST

PAY ATTENTION TO THE DETAILS:

- [ ] Vacuum and/or wash floors and carpet.
- [ ] Clean windows, mirrors, and light fixtures until shining.
- [ ] Wash marks off walls, baseboards, trim, light switches, doors, and hardware.
- [ ] Dust all surfaces.
- [ ] Decorate the bed to display a plush and luxurious look. Display bed linens (turned down neatly) to present lifestyle.
- [ ] Pick a monochromatic color scheme (if you can), because it evokes serenity. Add a limited number of neutral pillows to add warmth.
- [ ] Place wall hangings and pictures at eye level.
- [ ] Make sure the room is immaculate before every showing.
- [ ] If window treatments are a necessity, they should not distract from any potential view, be outdated, or dominate a room, (otherwise take them down to open up the room and maximize sunlight). If the view is becoming and not unsightly, open window treatments for every showing.

SELL, DONATE, OR STORE:

- [ ] Furniture not used for a specific purpose.
- [ ] Any and all dirty laundry (even if it is stored in hampers).
- [ ] Books, Bibles, magazines.
- [ ] Valuable items and collections.
- [ ] Personal items such as family photos, religious symbols, and personal hygiene products.
- [ ] Anything you wouldn't normally find in a bedroom, such as a treadmill.
- [ ] Any signs of pets such as food dishes, toys, or litter boxes.
- [ ] Any ash catchers, such as ashtrays or incense burners.

Notes:

CLOSETS AND LINEN SPACE STAGING CHECKLIST

PAY ATTENTION TO THE DETAILS:

- [ ] Clean shelving, interior walls, doors, and hardware.
- [ ] Keep floors vacuumed and clear with the exception of neatly arranged footwear.
- [ ] Hang clothes on hangers, with all items facing the same direction (wooden hangers if possible). Distribute clothing evenly along the rod to give the impression of plenty of space.
- [ ] Tidy small items you use daily by storing in baskets placed on shelves.
- [ ] Fold all items neatly and uniformly.
- [ ] Store bedding inside its matching pillowcase for neatness and ease of use.
- [ ] Coordinate linens by color.

SELL, DONATE, OR STORE:

- [ ] Items you haven't used within the past year (pack those you do not use on a regular basis).
- [ ] All items being stored in the space that don't normally belong in a closet.

Notes:

CURB APPEAL STAGING CHECKLIST

PAY ATTENTION TO THE DETAILS:

- [ ] Take down any forgotten past seasonal items (such as holiday decorations).
- [ ] Take a look at your house from across the street and see what you can do to make it more presentable.
- [ ] Clear away children's items and store them neatly behind the house, or in a shed.
- [ ] Put away any gardening tools, home improvement equipment, or similar materials.
- [ ] Mow the lawn and clear it of clippings, and make sure to remove any dead or dying plants.
- [ ] Dispose of litter.
- [ ] Remove animal droppings.
- [ ] Ensure buyers aren't at risk during winter months by keeping walkways shoveled and sanded.
- [ ] In the spring and summer, put down fresh mulch in flower beds.
- [ ] Ensure your lawn, walkways, flower beds, and driveways have a clean line with edging, or renew the look and remove the grass surrounding these areas.
- [ ] Use a good lawn fertilizer and weed killer, and water the grass well.
- [ ] Sweep driveways, decks, walkways, porches, etc.
- [ ] Clear out any moss and/or debris from roof, gutters, eavestroughs, and walkways.
- [ ] Open up the view, invite more sunlight in, and make sure walkways aren't obstructed, by trimming trees and bushes.
- [ ] Keep doors, windows, and window frames clean and clear of any moss or mold.
- [ ] Clean light fixtures.

SELL, DONATE, OR STORE:

- [ ] Any items that do not lend themselves to a simplified, showcased environment.
- [ ] Window screens and screen door (if possible).
- [ ] Boats, RVs, snowmobiles, watercrafts, ATVs, etc., (move to another location).
- [ ] Children's toys.

Notes:

SELF-COUNSEL PRESS — DO YOUR OWN HOME STAGING – AIII-5 08

DINING ROOM STAGING CHECKLIST

PAY ATTENTION TO THE DETAILS:

- ☐ Vacuum and/or wash floors and carpet.

- ☐ Wash marks off walls, baseboards, trim, light switches, doors, and hardware.

- ☐ Clean windows, mirrors, and light fixtures until shining.

- ☐ Clean and tidy table and chairs.

- ☐ Arrange any electronics.

- ☐ Rotate any rectangular or square tables so they are at an angle from the wall, to make the room feel more spacious and maximize traffic flow.

- ☐ Display a fresh flower arrangement in the center of the table.

- ☐ Create a small vignette of a bottle of wine, a few wine glasses, and a carafe on a hutch (if available).

- ☐ Keep wall hangings and pictures at eye level.

- ☐ Open window treatments for every showing (if drapes remain and the view is becoming and not unsightly). Window treatments should not distract from any potential view, be outdated, or dominate a room; otherwise take them down to depersonalize the space, open up the room, and maximize sunlight.

SELL, DONATE, OR STORE:

- ☐ Any furniture not used for a specific purpose.

- ☐ Any window treatments that aren't a necessity.

- ☐ Any fixtures not intended to stay in the home.

- ☐ Buffet off the hutch, to open up the space.

- ☐ Table leaves and additional chairs.

- ☐ Area rugs.

- ☐ Wall hangings and pictures (set aside only one large picture per wall, or a group of three smaller pictures).

- ☐ Any valuable items and collections.

- ☐ Personal items such as family photos, religious symbols, etc.

☐ Anything you wouldn't normally find in a dining room, such as a desk.

☐ Any signs of pets such as food dishes, toys, or litter boxes.

☐ Any ash catchers such as ashtrays or incense burners.

Notes:

FAMILY OR GREAT ROOM STAGING CHECKLIST

PAY ATTENTION TO THE DETAILS:

☐ Vacuum and/or wash floors and carpet.

☐ Wash marks off walls, baseboards, trim, light switches, doors, and hardware.

☐ Clean windows, mirrors, and light fixtures until shining.

☐ Dust any televisions, radios, stereos, computer, and any other electronics.

☐ Dust and clean all other surfaces.

☐ Clean every detail of the fireplace or woodstove to show care, and that it is free of any potential fire hazard.

☐ Keep wall hangings and pictures at eye level.

☐ Open window treatments for every showing (if drapes remain and the view is becoming and not unsightly).

☐ Arrange a limited number of neutral pillows to add a warm look and feel to the room.

☐ Play soft music (but only if it is coordinated with other rooms, if universal music is not available).

SELL, DONATE OR STORE:

☐ Any furniture not used for a specific purpose.

☐ Any window treatments that aren't a necessity (they should not distract from any potential view, be outdated, or dominate a room. Otherwise, take them down to depersonalize the space, open up the room, and maximize sunlight).

☐ Children's toys and games.

☐ Wall hangings and pictures (set aside only one large picture per wall or a group of three smaller pictures).

☐ Two-thirds of everything stored on bookshelves. Display remaining items in an organized and attractive way.

☐ Any valuable items and collections.

☐ Personal items such as family photos, religious symbols, etc.

☐   Any ash catchers such as ashtrays or incense burners.

☐   Any items stored under furniture.

Notes:

FRONT ENTRANCE STAGING CHECKLIST

PAY ATTENTION TO THE DETAILS:

- [ ] Vacuum and/or wash floors and carpet.
- [ ] Wash marks off walls, baseboards, trim, light switches, doors, and hardware.
- [ ] Clean windows, mirrors, and light fixtures until shining.
- [ ] Dust all surfaces.
- [ ] Keep wall hangings and pictures at eye level.
- [ ] Remove window treatments.
- [ ] Ensure furniture does not hinder traffic flow.
- [ ] Hang coats on similar hangers arranged in the same direction, and hide small items in baskets.
- [ ] Determine if there are any odors to get rid of. Ask someone who doesn't live in the home to help (it is likely you may not smell anything because you are used to it).

SELL, DONATE, OR STORE:

- [ ] Any furniture not used for a specific purpose.
- [ ] Any fixtures not intended to stay in the home.
- [ ] Any valuable items or collections.
- [ ] Personal items such as family photos, religious symbols, etc.
- [ ] Area rugs.
- [ ] Anything you wouldn't normally find in an entranceway, such as items to be returned to stores, toys, etc.
- [ ] Any signs of pets such as food dishes, toys, or litter boxes.
- [ ] Any items on tables and shelves (e.g., keys and other "drop off" items).
- [ ] Boots, shoes, ball caps, and any seasonal items.

Notes:

GARAGE STAGING CHECKLIST

PAY ATTENTION TO THE DETAILS:

- [ ] Sweep and clean the floors.
- [ ] Ensure walls are relatively clean.
- [ ] Store garbage neatly and remove any odors.
- [ ] Ensure windows, doors, hardware, light switches, and fixtures are clean and functioning properly.
- [ ] Arrange required items neatly on shelves in containers for a neat appearance.
- [ ] Remove any spiderwebs or telltale signs of insects of any kind.
- [ ] Ensure all chemicals are properly stored in bins, high on shelves.
- [ ] Keep the door into the house closed (if possible).
- [ ] Keep garage doors down or closed at all times.

SELL, DONATE, OR STORE:

- [ ] Any items not being used on a daily basis, such as sports equipment or seasonal items.
- [ ] Any items not usually stored in a garage, such as Aunt Susan's old tea cart that you promised to refinish one day.
- [ ] Tools and equipment that can't be displayed to add to the lifestyle you wish to portray.
- [ ] Any toxic supplies (put in plastic storage bins with lids, and put high on a shelf out of harm's way). Empty paint cans and/or other toxic containers can be taken to your local environmental depot.

Notes:

HALLWAYS/STAIRWAYS STAGING CHECKLIST

PAY ATTENTION TO THE DETAILS:

☐ Clean floors, walls, and baseboards.

☐ Clean windows and doors until sparkling.

☐ Ensure nothing prevents easy passage.

SELL, DONATE, OR STORE:

☐ All items, such as any furniture, wall hangings, pictures, runners, etc.

Notes:

SELF-COUNSEL PRESS — DO YOUR OWN HOME STAGING – AIII-10 08

KITCHEN STAGING CHECKLIST

PAY ATTENTION TO THE DETAILS:

- [ ] Clean and polish floors, any stainless steel, reflective surfaces, and/or tiles.
- [ ] Ensure every detail of *every* appliance sparkles.
- [ ] Wipe down walls and baseboards.
- [ ] Ensure all glass, fixtures, faucets, and windows glisten.
- [ ] Dust and clean the top of all cupboards.
- [ ] Renew wood surfaces by applying appropriate products.
- [ ] Clean all hardware, especially cabinet doorknobs and drawer pulls.
- [ ] Clean backsplash; if tiled, bleach and reapply sealer.
- [ ] Keep the kitchen sink clean and empty on a daily basis.
- [ ] Prevent odors by emptying trash and compost daily.
- [ ] Keep the inside of cupboards clean and tidy.
- [ ] Arrange any square or rectangular table on an angle so that it appears to be the smallest it can be to create more space.
- [ ] Display a fresh flower arrangement on the table, or a bowl of fruit on the counter.
- [ ] Open drapes for every open house or showing, if you choose not to put them in storage.

SELL, DONATE, OR STORE:

- [ ] Any furniture not used for a specific purpose.
- [ ] Window coverings (if view permits), to maximize light in the room.
- [ ] Any valuable items or collections.
- [ ] Personal items such as family photos, religious symbols, etc.
- [ ] Area rugs (they create an invisible barrier — with the exception of using only one to distract from dated or unsightly floor patterns).
- [ ] Anything you wouldn't normally find in a kitchen, such as items to be returned to stores, etc.
- [ ] Any signs of pets such as food dishes, toys, or litter boxes.
- [ ] Trash cans and compost bins.

- ☐ Cleaning supplies (store securely and out of reach).

- ☐ Any items kept on any surfaces, such as items on tables, window ledges, countertops, etc.

- ☐ Dish towels, dish cloths, and oven mitts.

- ☐ Remove any counter appliances, such as coffee makers, can openers, televisions, radios, etc.

- ☐ Knives and other sharp objects (store high and out of sight).

- ☐ Refrigerator "stuff," it should be clear of everything (magnets, children's art, etc.).

- ☐ Any cooking ingredients.

- ☐ Any fixtures not intended to stay in the home when it sells.

- ☐ Any added shelving or cabinets. It may give the impression there is not enough storage space in the kitchen cupboards.

Notes:

LAUNDRY ROOM STAGING CHECKLIST

PAY ATTENTION TO THE DETAILS:

☐ Clean floors, walls, windows, baseboards, trim, light switches, fixtures, and hardware.

☐ Do the laundry, and place dirty laundry in the washer, or put in a nice hamper to clear the area.

☐ Clear dryer lint tray to indicate good care and not imply any fire hazards.

☐ Keep both the washer and dryer clean and looking virtually new.

☐ Keep workspace clear of any clutter, clothes, and/or garbage.

☐ Arrange appliances and create a work space to appear like a laundry room, if laundry room is in an unfinished basement. Ensure it feels like a room and not just a washer and dryer placed in a basement.

☐ Light area well, it opens up the space and buyers feel more comfortable.

☐ Empty garbage bin.

SELL, DONATE, OR STORE:

☐ Any empty containers that are not currently being used or are almost empty.

☐ All items from countertops.

☐ Any excess laundry supplies (keep out of sight).

☐ Any remaining laundry that needs to be put away.

☐ Anything not usually found in a laundry room.

☐ Anything hanging on a laundry line (and the line itself).

☐ Any signs of pets such as food dishes, toys, or litter boxes.

Notes:

LIVING ROOM STAGING CHECKLIST

PAY ATTENTION TO THE DETAILS:

- [ ] Vacuum and/or wash floors and carpet.

- [ ] Wash marks off walls, baseboards, trim, light switches, doors, and hardware.

- [ ] Clean windows, mirrors, and light fixtures until shining.

- [ ] Dust and clean all surfaces.

- [ ] Arrange televisions, radios, stereos, computer, and any other electronics.

- [ ] Clean every detail of the fireplace or woodstove to show care, and to not imply any potential fire hazards.

- [ ] Arrange a limited number of neutral pillows to add a warm look and feel to the room.

- [ ] Keep wall hangings and pictures at eye level.

- [ ] Open window treatments for every showing (if drapes remain and the view is becoming and not unsightly).

- [ ] Play soft music (but only if it is coordinated with other rooms, if universal music is not available).

SELL, DONATE OR STORE:

- [ ] Any furniture not used for a specific purpose.

- [ ] If window treatments are a necessity, they should not distract from any potential view, be outdated, or dominate a room; otherwise, take them down to depersonalize the space, open up the room, and maximize sunlight.

- [ ] Children's toys and games.

- [ ] Wall hangings and pictures (set aside only one large picture, or a group of three smaller pictures per wall).

- [ ] Two-thirds of everything stored on bookshelves (display remaining items in an organized and attractive way.

- [ ] Any valuable items and collections.

- [ ] Personal items such as family photos, religious symbols, etc.

- [ ] Anything you wouldn't normally find in a living room, such as a treadmill.

- [ ] Any signs of pets such as food dishes, toys, or litter boxes.

☐ Any ash catchers such as ashtrays or incense burners.

☐ Any items stored under furniture.

☐ Any fixtures not intended to stay in the home once it sells.

Notes:

OFFICE STAGING CHECKLIST

PAY ATTENTION TO THE DETAILS:

- [ ] Clean carpets, walls, trim, baseboards, light switches, fixtures, windows, and doors.
- [ ] Arrange electronics.
- [ ] Keep computer turned off for all showings.
- [ ] Keep wall hangings and pictures at eye level.
- [ ] Ensure personal information is put away.

SELL, DONATE, OR STORE:

- [ ] Two-thirds of everything on bookshelves (display remaining items in an organized and attractive way).
- [ ] Any work-related items not used daily.
- [ ] Any electronics not used daily.
- [ ] Neatly arrange cords in use.
- [ ] Any personal items.

Notes:

REC ROOM/GAMES ROOM STAGING CHECKLIST

PAY ATTENTION TO THE DETAILS:

☐ Clean carpets, walls, trim, baseboards, light switches, fixtures, windows, and doors.

☐ Keep every detail of woodstoves or fireplaces spotless, to show care and to not imply any fire hazards.

☐ Keep window frames and windowpanes clean and clear of any mold and/or mildew.

☐ Keep any computer areas clean and free of clutter and wires.

☐ Arrange furnishings to display a lifestyle of fun and leisure.

☐ Add a limited number of neutral pillows for a warm look and feel.

☐ Open window treatments for every showing (if the view is becoming and not unsightly).

☐ Keep wall hangings and pictures at eye level.

SELL, DONATE, OR STORE:

☐ Any items not lending themselves to a simplified, showcased environment.

☐ Any special collections, or any expensive or personal items, such as family photos, religious items, etc.

☐ Any unnecessary, outdated, or dominating window treatments (to open up the room and maximize sunlight).

☐ Anything sitting on tables (except a lamp, and one discreet item).

☐ Window screens.

☐ Any ash catchers such as ashtrays or incense burners.

☐ Children's toys and games.

☐ Two-thirds of items currently displayed on bookshelves.

☐ Wall hangings and pictures (set aside only one large picture, or a group of three smaller pictures per wall).

- [ ] Unsightly electrical cords and wires.
- [ ] Items on mantels and hearths (keep only a few necessary items).

Notes:

YARD STAGING CHECKLIST

PAY ATTENTION TO THE DETAILS:

- [ ] Sweep decks, walks, porches, etc.
- [ ] Ensure buyers aren't at risk during winter months, by keeping walkways shoveled and sanded.
- [ ] Mow the lawn, keep it healthy, and clear it of any clippings. Remove any dead or dying plants.
- [ ] Use a good lawn fertilizer and weed killer, and water the grass well.
- [ ] Dispose of any litter.
- [ ] Remove animal droppings.
- [ ] Put away the garden hose and any gardening tools.
- [ ] Clear away children's items and store neatly behind the house (if not in a shed).
- [ ] Trim trees and bushes to open up the view and invite more sunlight in.
- [ ] Keep doors and windows clean.
- [ ] Keep window frames clear of any moss or mold.
- [ ] Clear out any moss and/or debris from roof, gutters, and walkways.
- [ ] Clean light fixtures to shine brighter.
- [ ] Create a fun lifestyle with outdoor furniture (an extension of the house).

SELL, DONATE, OR STORE:

- [ ] Old barbeques and used charcoal.
- [ ] Children's toys.
- [ ] Any items not being used or lending themselves to creating a setting of a simplified lifestyle.
- [ ] Window screens (if possible).
- [ ] Construction materials.

Notes: